An essential guide to becoming the consumate rhythm guitarist

by Charles Chapman

Cover Photo: Headstock of Benedetto "Renaissance Series" Il Palissandro Serial #37096.
Photo credit: John Bender

1 2 3 4 5 6 7 8 9 0

Visit us on the Web at www.melbay.com — E-mail us at email@melbay.com

TABLE OF CONTENTS

FOREWORD

The rhythm guitarist who can play the appropriate chord voicing that fits the style and blends with the musical situation is a rare commodity. The novice is generally only aware of 2 or 3 inversions and most likely are in the same category or "chord family". Stylizing your chords and being able to fit them into different situations is really what *Rhythm Guitar Tutor* is all about. An added benefit is improved technical prowess of both right and left hands while gaining an appreciation of many other rhythm guitar styles that here-to-fore many have not been exposed to.

The chords are divided into four basic categories that provide diverse distinctive sounds. When actually performing, you will probably want to "mix and match" to fit the situation, but it is good to initially work on each identity separately developing the sound and technique for each. Sub categories could go on forever, but the ones in this text give you the "meat and potatoes" to get the job done.

Most guitarists are mainly concerned with lead and melody oriented material without realizing that the foundation of all music is harmony. Get accustomed to the manner in which these chords sound, feel, and stylistically fit the examples. The ability to play rhythm guitar is not only fun but also lucrative. I can guarantee that guitarists who play rhythm guitar well will never be out of work.

Symbols Used In Text

O = open string

1, 2, 3, 4 = fingers of the left hand

X = do not play (mute)

⊓ = Down stroke of pick

V = Up stroke of pick

Voicing = Another term for chord shape or form. All three terms can be used interchangeably.

R = Root (note chord is named after)

AR = Assumed Root —When a chord does not contain a root (not unusual) the assumed root will only be for a reference point.

RIGHT-HAND PICK TECHNIQUE

This text is intended to be played with a flat pick although most examples can be executed with an open right-hand as well. The type of pick or plectrum you use can vary according to your playing style and personal preference, I recommend the Fender heavy pick (style 351). This pick is not too large or small and is generally a comfortable fit to all size hands. The heavy pick is easier to execute dynamics and also projects a rounder and richer tone than the thinner varieties.

There are many different schools of thought on holding the pick, but the general consensus is that your index finger should be running parallel to your thumb and the strings. The pick should be held between the thumb and index finger with only enough pick exposed to strike the strings. The fingers of the right-hand should be lightly flexed into a fist eliminating "finger drag" that can slow down right-hand technique.

Proper Pick Position in Right Hand

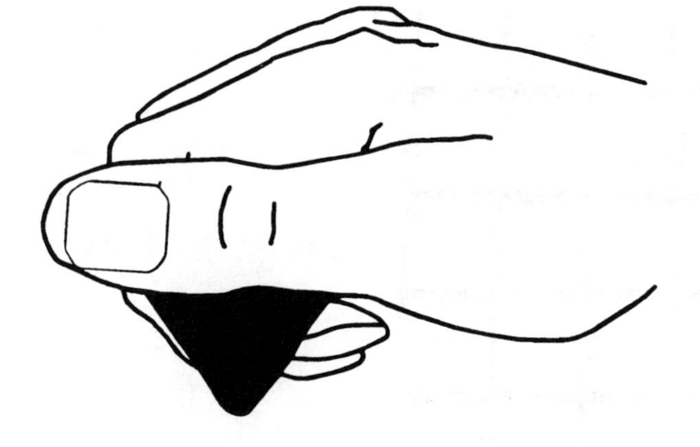

Standard Size Pick

When using a pick, motion comes from a combination of the elbow and slight motion at the wrist. Down and up strokes use the elbows motion and a wrist motion similar to turning a key in a door.

"Always remember that the pick is like a paintbrush that can create fine or bold strokes. The pick or right-hand fingers are the most critical parts of musical expression for the guitar".

Bill Purse—Guitar Chair Duquesne University

FINGERBOARD CHART

The chart below is vital to understanding the inner working of chord structures and most importantly recognizing the proper placement of chord root notes. I suggest you copy and have this chart readily available when practicing.

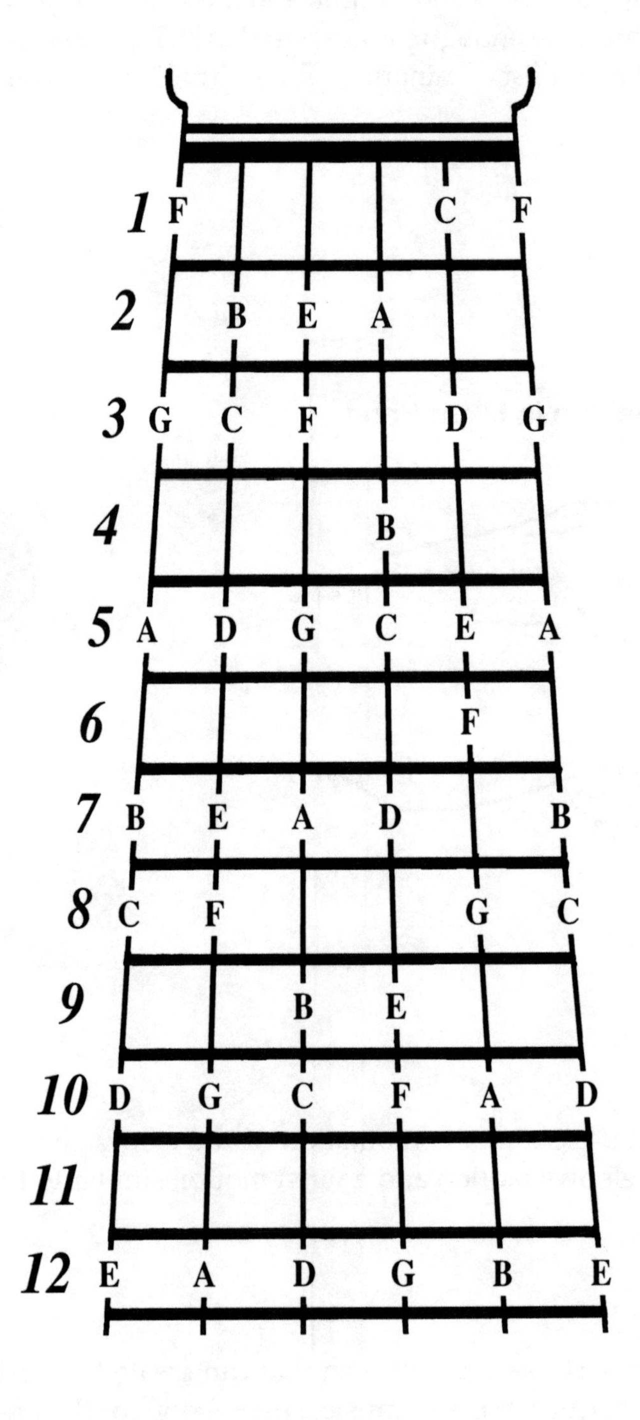

Chapter I

DESCRIPTIONS AND DIAGRAMS

Folk Chords

Open string first position chord forms are very distinctive and by and large, the most widely used. The term folk is synonymous as guitarists in this genre use these voicings extensively.

Folk chords are generally considered elementary because they are the easiest to finger and are the first chords taught, but have a unique quality that is often desired. They produce a legato quality and power that can't be duplicated (especially on acoustic or acoustic 12 string.) They are a part of our sound palette and should be given their appropriate place in our arsenal of available chord voicings.

The following are the most common:

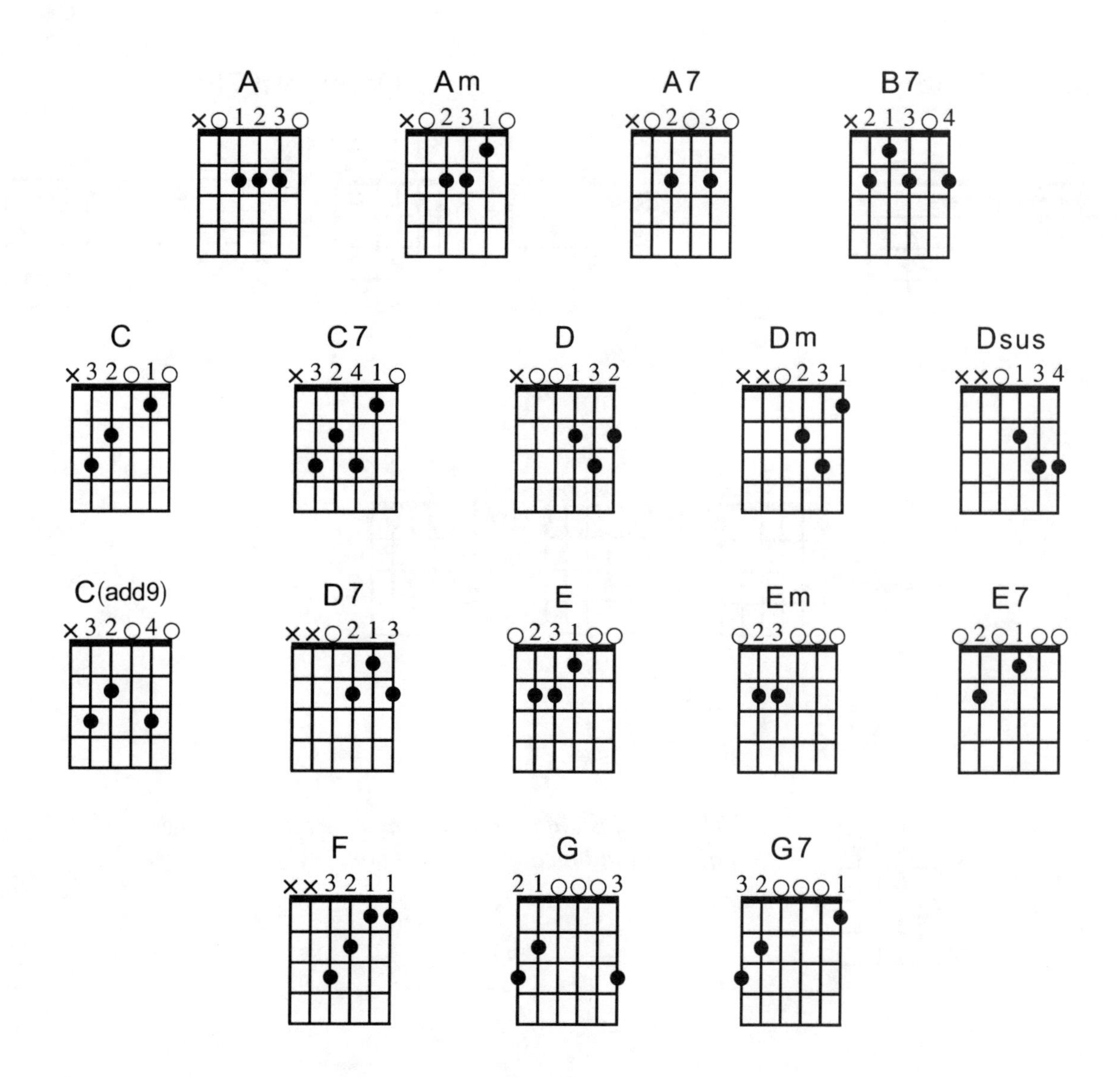

DESCRIPTIONS AND DIAGRAMS

Utility Chords

These voicings are referred to as utility chords because they are functional in most musical situations. They often sound best in the rock and blues genre or when performing without a bass player.

Note that these chord forms can be somewhat cumbersome and are generally not the best choice for a big band or a jazz situation where a bass player is present.

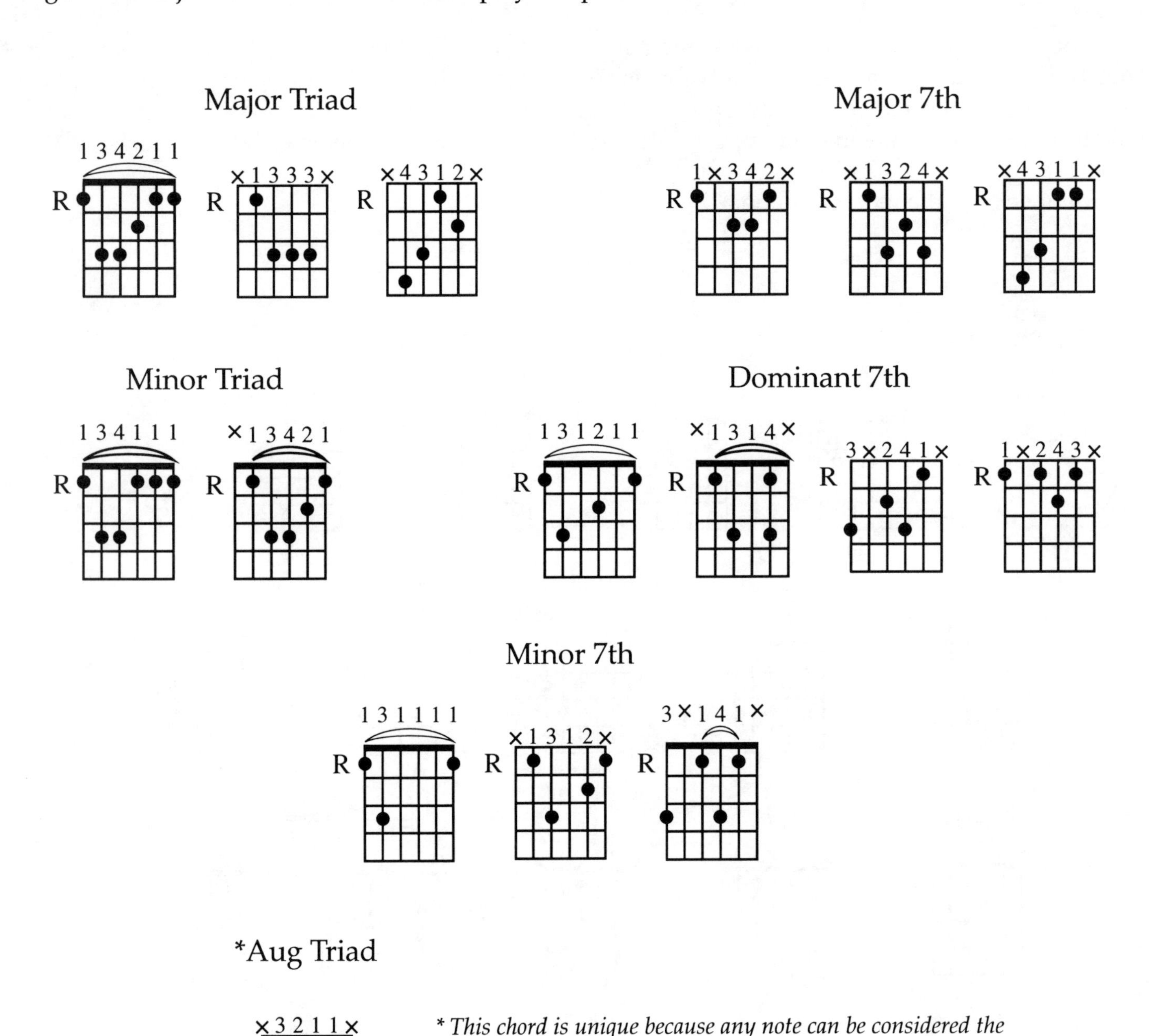

** This chord is unique because any note can be considered the root. It can function as three distinct Augmented triads.*

R = *Indicates the chord root or the note the chord is named after*

DESCRIPTIONS AND DIAGRAMS

Utility Chords—con't

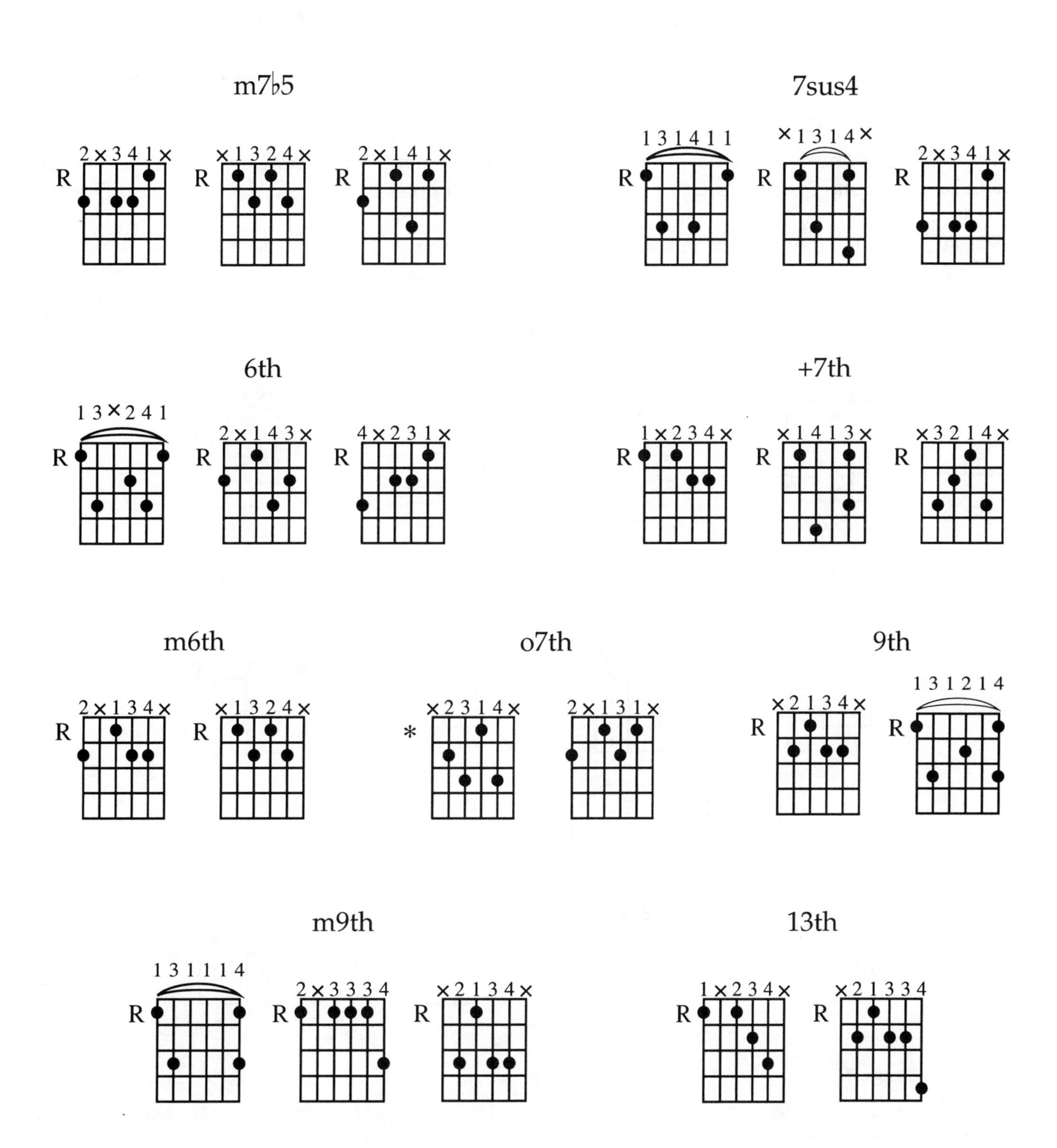

This chord is unique because any note can be the root. It can function as four different diminished 7th chords.

DESCRIPTIONS AND DIAGRAMS

Drop -2

Without getting into musical technicalities, Drop-2 is basically playing chord forms on four adjacent strings, avoiding or muting the other two strings. The most common string sets are the first four and middle four sets of strings. We do not use the bottom four because they can tend to sound dark and dissonant.

These chord forms are exactly what is called for when performing in the chord-melody style and especially in jazz *comping. For Drop-2 to provide the optimum potential, a bass player should be present.

The following are the most common Drop-2 voicings on strings 1, 2, 3, 4.

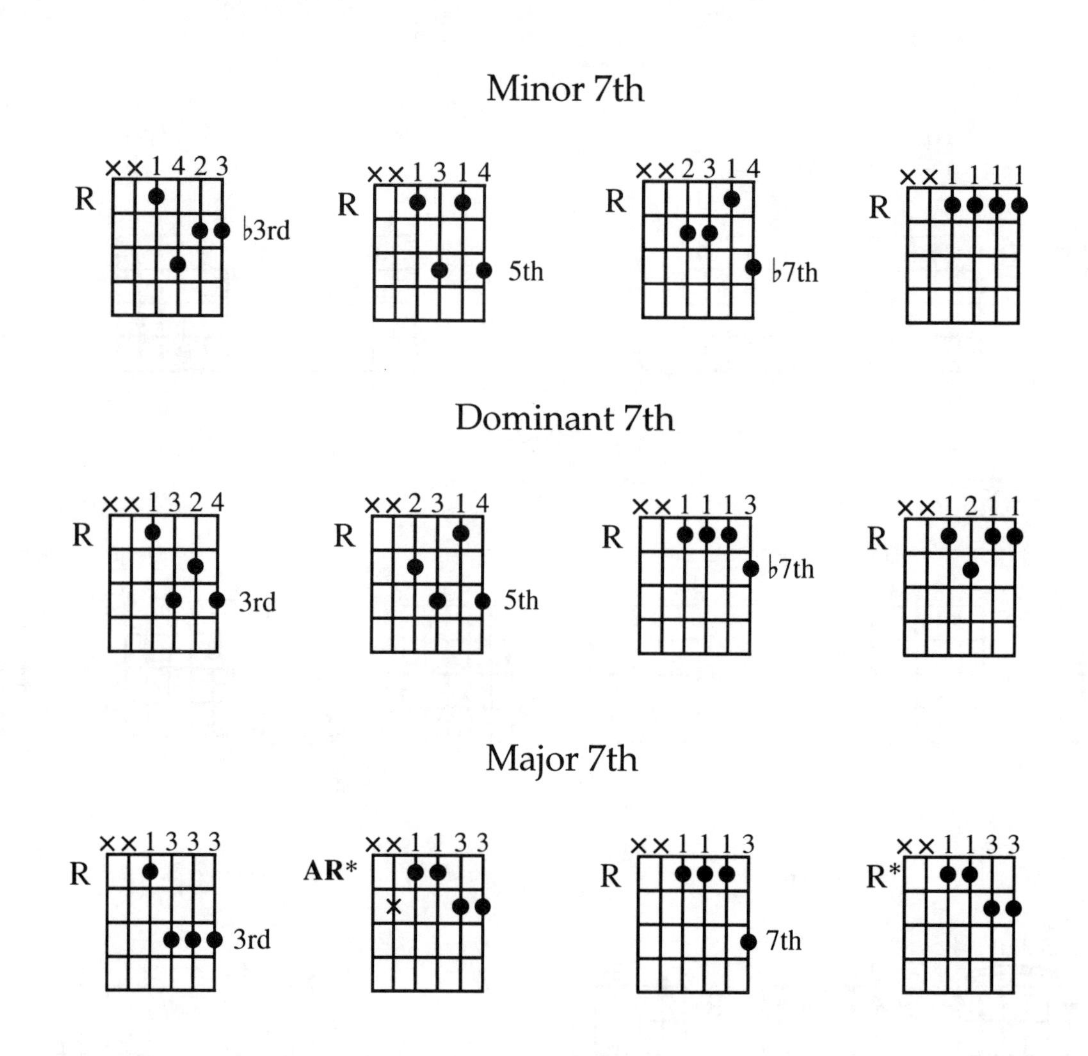

comping = To compliment. Rhythm guitarist should listen to the lead and rest of the rhythm section and perform chords and rhythms that fits the mood and style of the tune.

* = *The 6/9 chord can generally be be substituted for a major 7 when the fingering or chord sound is not appropropiate for the situation.*

AR = *Is an abbreviation for assumed root. A chord structure does not have to have the root to sound the appropriate harmonic sonority. By indicating the AR it provides a reference point making it easier to remember and find in different locations on the fingerboard.*

DESCRIPTIONS AND DIAGRAMS

Drop-2 —con't

The following are the Drop-2 chords on string sets 2, 3, 4, 5:

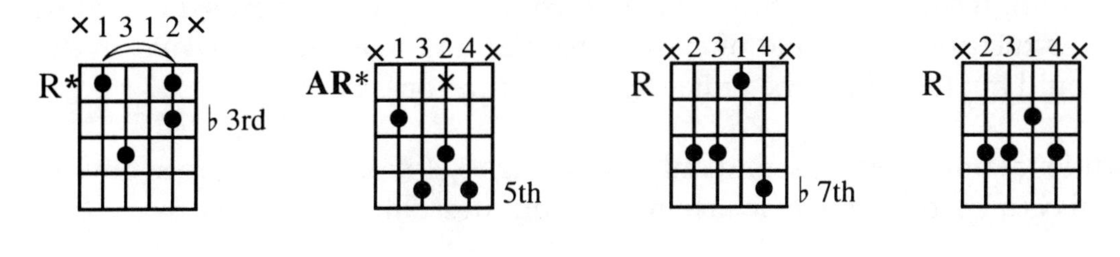

Dominant 7th

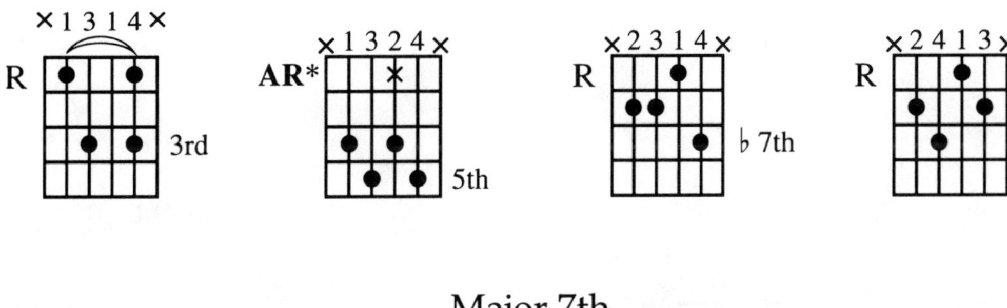

Major 7th

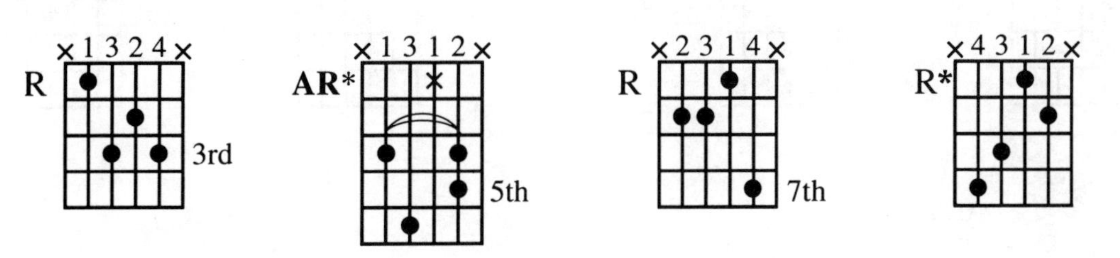

For these chord forms, it is advantageous to be aware of the chord tone that is in the lead (melody or highest note) as well as where the lowest note would be. Even though this involves quite a bit of thought, it will be beneficial when attempting chord-melody performance.

* = *Often a substitution will be used for either ease of fingering or desired sound.*

DESCRIPTIONS AND DIAGRAMS

Freddie Green Chords

When the Freddie Green chords are asked for it is generally dealing with the rhythm style of time playing. Time playing is the "four-to-the-bar rhythm-style associated with the big bands of the '40s and '50's.

Freddie Green is the guitarist most associated with this style and performed with the Count Basie big band from 1937 until his death in 1987. Instead of using large utility chords, he used mostly two and three note chord structures. He would often reharmonize and masterfully weave around the bass line so the listener could not tell where the guitar left off and the bass began.

To get this traditional time playing sound only use strings 3, 4 & 6. Freddie Green obviously used more than this, but this is an excellent way to achieve that quintessential sound.

These chord voicings sound great with a big band and can also work well when performing with a keyboard player.

The following are the most common:

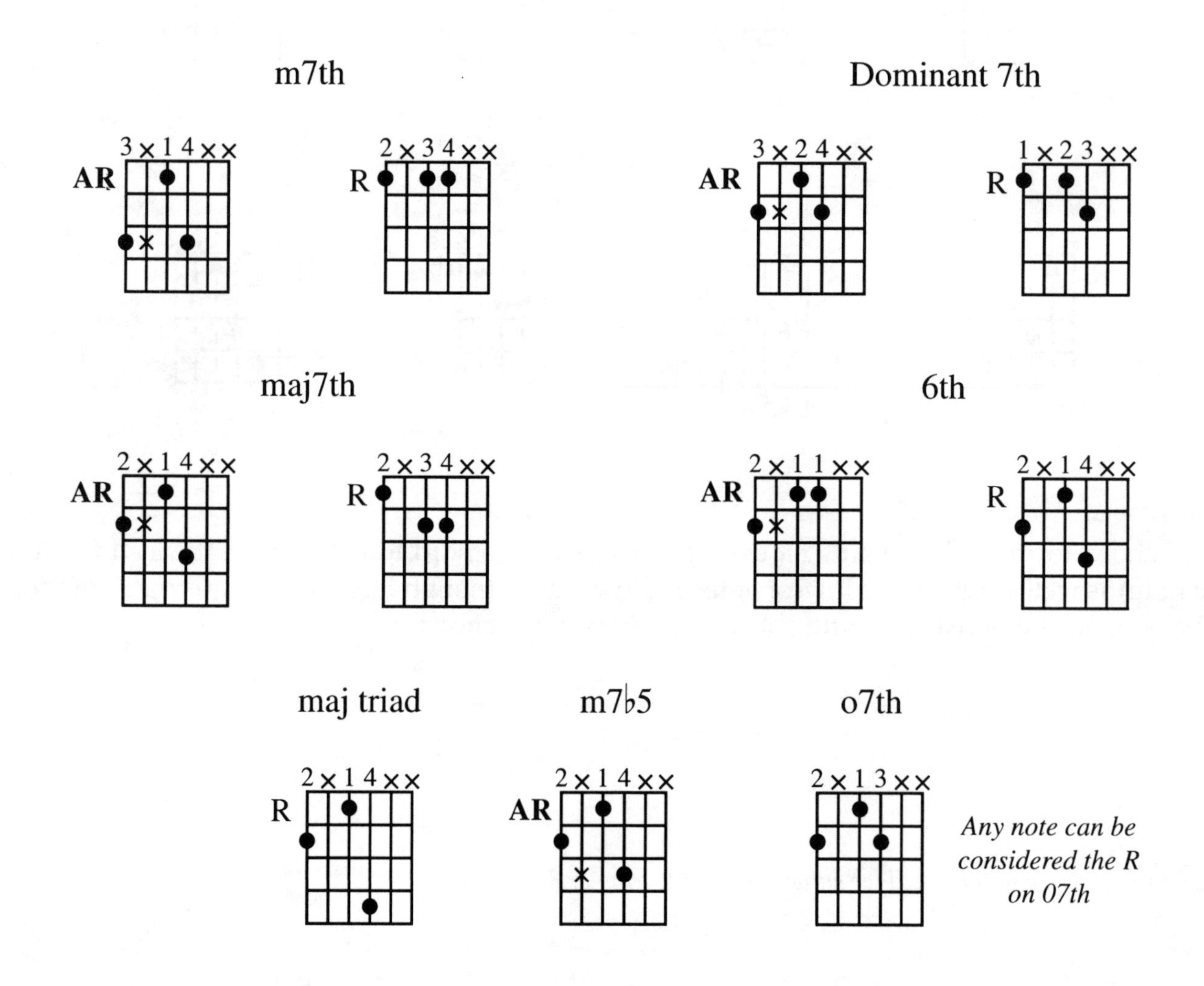

Chapter II

MUSICAL MARKINGS & READING TIPS

Dynamics

Dynamics and articulations are often omitted in lead sheets or by amateur musicians. The general rule is when none are present, the music is performed as the style dictates. I personally feel this sometimes leaves too much for the individual musician to interpret.

The following is a list of dynamics that the contemporary musician must know and be able to use correctly. Tradition dictates that the Italian terms for dynamics be used.

Term	Abbreviation	Translation
pianissimo	*pp*	very soft
piano	*p*	soft
mezzo-piano	*mp*	medium soft
mezzo-forte	*mf*	medium loud
forte	*f*	loud
fortissimo	*ff*	very loud

Always use abbreviations, never the full name; also, lower case letters are always used rather that capitals. Dynamics should always be placed beneath the staff, directly below or slightly to the left of the first note. Once a dynamic level is indicated it is maintained until a new one appears.

**Dynamics — Words or signs indicating degrees or changes of loudness.*

MUSICAL MARKINGS & READING TIPS

Dynamics

To indicate a gradual increase or decrease in volume, the following terms may be used:

Term	Abbreviation	Translation
crescendo	cresc.	increase in volume
diminuendo	dim.	decrease in volume
decrescendo	decresc.	decrease in volume

Diminuendo and decrescendo mean the same and are interchangeable. I personally prefer to use decrescendo.

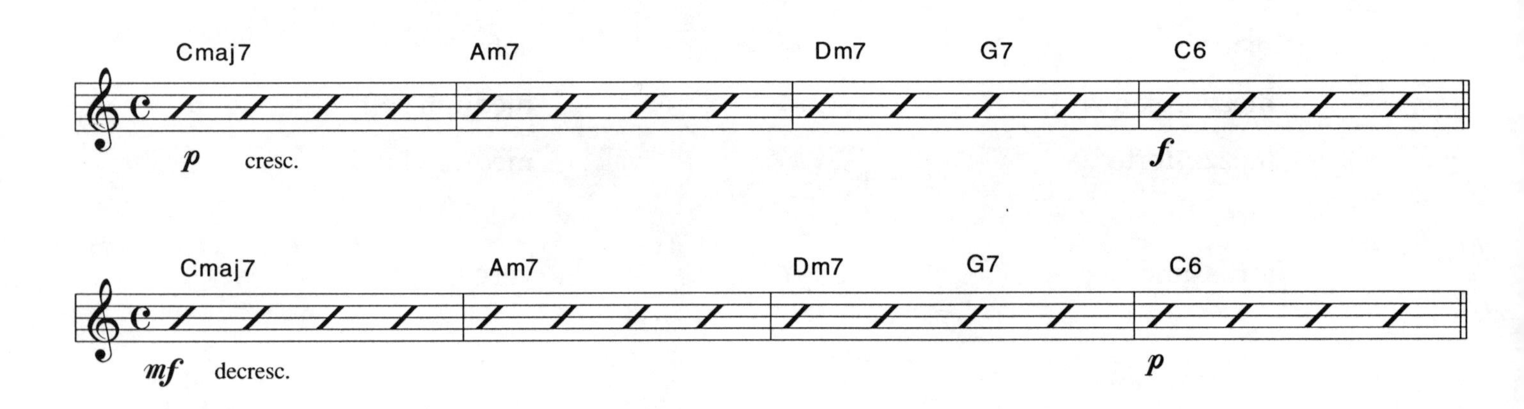

To indicate a gradual increase or decrease in volume for a short duration, "wedges" are used instead of verbal terms.

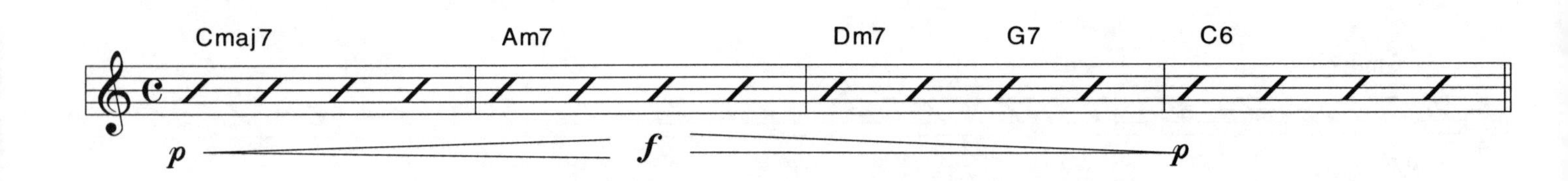

MUSICAL MARKINGS & READING TIPS

Repeats

The repeat sign consists of a double bar and two dots as follows:

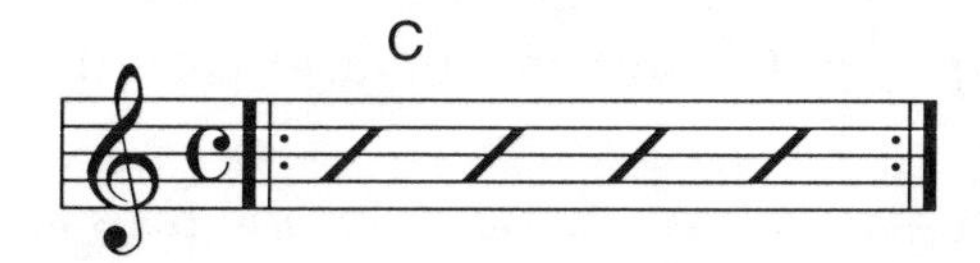

The general rule governing repeat signs is that you repeat back to the nearest repeat sign facing the opposite direction. If there is not a repeat sign facing the opposite direction, return to the beginning of the piece.

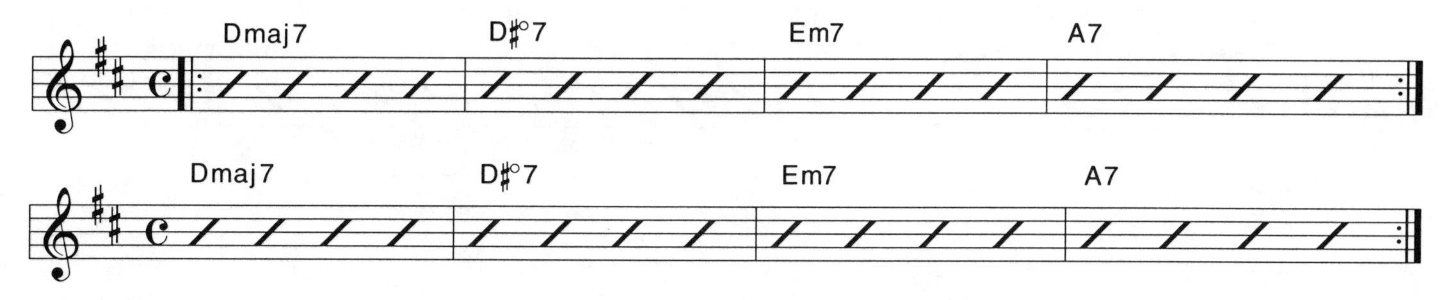

Both of the above examples notate the exact same music. I personally use repeat signs on both end as I find it the best way to avoid confusion.

The single measure repeat sign is another notational shortcut. This symbol instructs the performer to repeat the previous measure once.

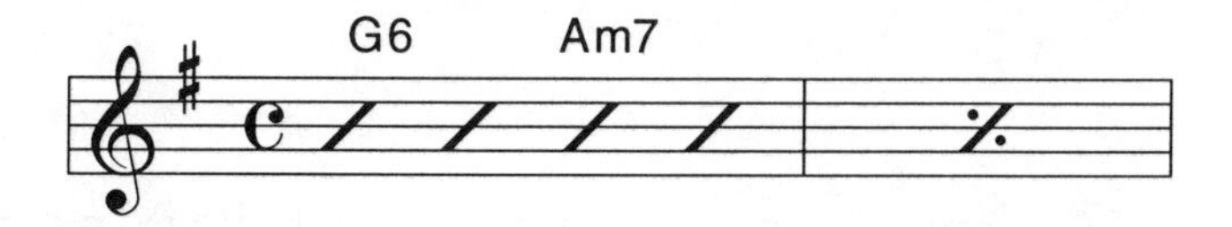

If more than one measure is to be repeated, indicate above the measure the number of previous measures that are to be repeated.

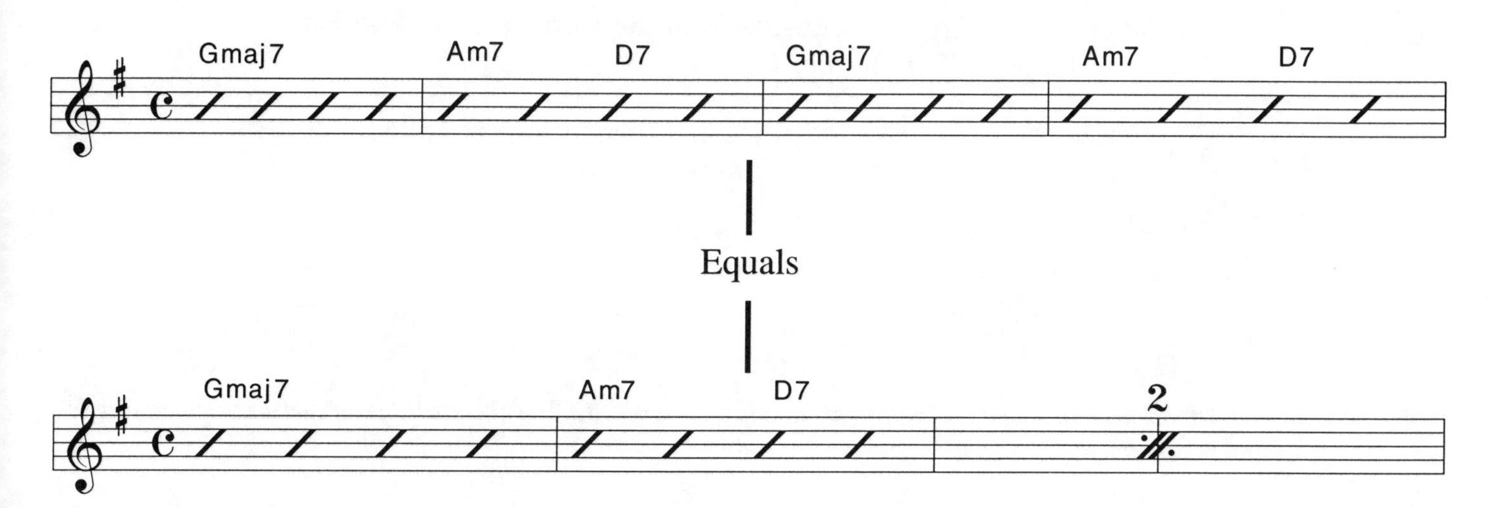

MUSICAL MARKINGS & READING TIPS

Repeats & Tempo Indications

First and second endings are a musical shortcut that can save a great deal of writing and paper. It indicates the first time you play to the repeat sign, then return to the beginning of the section that is to be repeated. The second time you skip the first ending and play the second ending.

A 1st or 2nd ending does not necessarily have to be only one measure long. Endings can be any length within reason.

If an exact tempo is critical to a piece of music, a *metronome marking should be used.

Rock Ballad ♩ mm =100	This indicates that the tempo is equal to one hundred quarter notes per minute.

While the usual notation indicates how many times a quater note beats per minute, for fast tempos or unusual time signatures, other note values can be used.

mm 𝅗𝅥 =100	This indicates that there are one hundred half notes per minute.
mm 𝅗𝅥. = 60	This indicates that there are sixty dotted half notes per minute.

**Metronome — An apparatus that sounds regular beats at adjustable speeds. The abbreviation for metronome marking is "mm" and is usually placed beside the stylistic indicator.*

MUSICAL MARKINGS & READING TIPS

Articulations

The three most common articulations are staccato (.), legato (—), and accent (>).

Staccato indicates that the note should be played short. A good way to visualize this is to think of the note as being "hot" and to get off it as quickly as possible. It is indicated by a dot above the staff and generally applied to notes with a duration of one beat or less.

Legato means to play the note as smoothly as possible, usually with a soft dull attack. The symbol for legato is a dash over the note. The general rule is, if there are no articulations present, the notes are assumed to be played legato.

An accent indicates that the note should receive an emphasized attack. The duration of the note is not altered and the accent is drawn as a small wedge over the note affected.

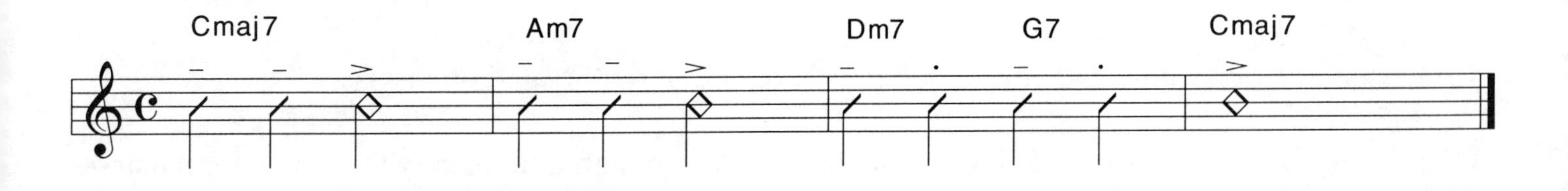

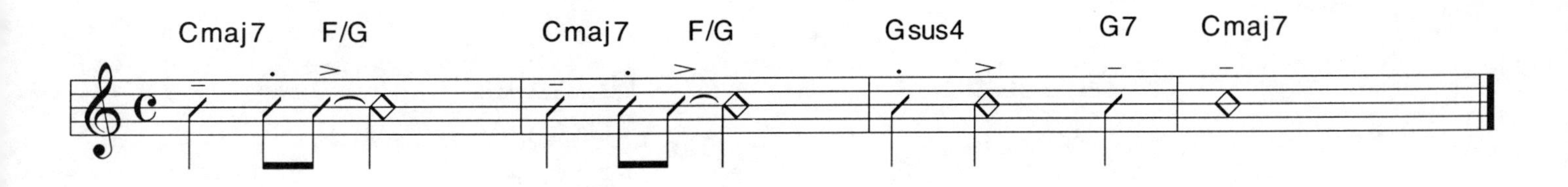

**Articulation — A term used to denote (demand) clarity and distinct rendition musical performance, whether vocal or instrumental. Correct breathing, phrasing, attack, legato, and staccato are some of the aspects involved with articulations.*

MUSICAL MARKINGS & READING TIPS

Short Cuts

Many times charts and lead sheets utilize short cuts such as repeats, endings, etc. The following short-cuts are what I consider to be the most common.

Fine = The End

D.𝄋 = Play from sign (𝄋)

D.C. = Play from the beginning

D.𝄋 (S.R.) = Play from the sign without repeats

D.𝄋 (C.R.) = Play from the sign without repeats

D.C. (S.R.) = Play from the beginning without repeats

D.C. (C.R.) = Play from the beginning with repeats

D.C. al Fine = Go to the beginning and stop at Fine

V.S. = Turn Page

Unwritten Rule: Play only 2nd endings after D. 𝄋 or D.C. if not notated otherwise.

Often it will be hard to locate a D.S., Coda or Fine, so I like to highlight them with a fluorescent marker. These musical shorts cuts can be very disconcerting to the musician and are only there to save paper and copying time. In most traditional literature, repeats and musical shortcuts do not exist because it tends to break the flow and concentration of the performer.

Abbreviation	Derivation
D.C.	Da Capo
D.𝄋	Sal Signo
S.R.	Senza Repeats
C.R.	Con Repeats
V.S.	Volti Subito

MUSICAL MARKINGS & READING TIPS

Miscellaneous Markings

Fine = The End

Segue = Continue on without stopping

V.S. = Turn page (usually have at least one measure rest on following page)

V.S. Quickly = Turn page quickly (generally only 1 or 2 beats of rest)

V.S. No Time = Turn page (there is no silence and you are up to your own devices how you are going to do it.

Fermata and Caesura

The proper name is fermata, however, it is commonly referred to as a "hold" or "birdseye". It instructs the player to hold a note or rest until cued to continue. The caesura commonly referred to as "railroad tracks" or a "cut" sign indicates that the musician should immediately stop playing and not continued until cued. These symbols are generally only used in studio or orchestra context where a conductor is present. The exception is on solo pieces where the performer may use their discretion.

Often the fermata is used in conjunction with a caesura

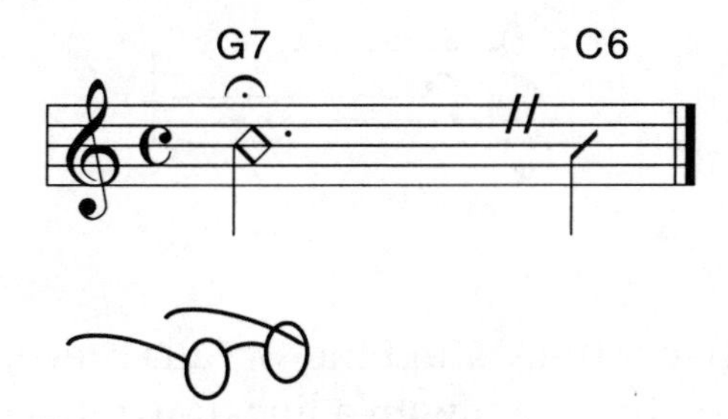

The eyeglasses means there is a section that could be misleading, awkward or abnormally difficult. I do not know if this is standarized, but have seen this "penciled in"* on parts I have recieved in both studio and theater parts all over the country.

**Pencilled in = when a performer writes on the score so he or she can remember something when they get to that section. Marking a piece of music is not the norm, but is acceptable if it can be helpful in executing the part for either you or future guitarists perform this particular piece of music.*

MUSICAL MARKINGS & READING TIPS

Time Signatures

The time signature appears directly after the clef and the key signature. The time signature consists of two numbers vertically aligned. It is placed only at the beginning of the piece or when the time changes. When the time signature changes, there is no need to use a new clef unless that is changing also. The upper number instructs how may beats in each measure and the lower indicates the chosen unit of measurement (half note, quarter note, etc.).

Listed below are common time signatures seen in contemporary music:

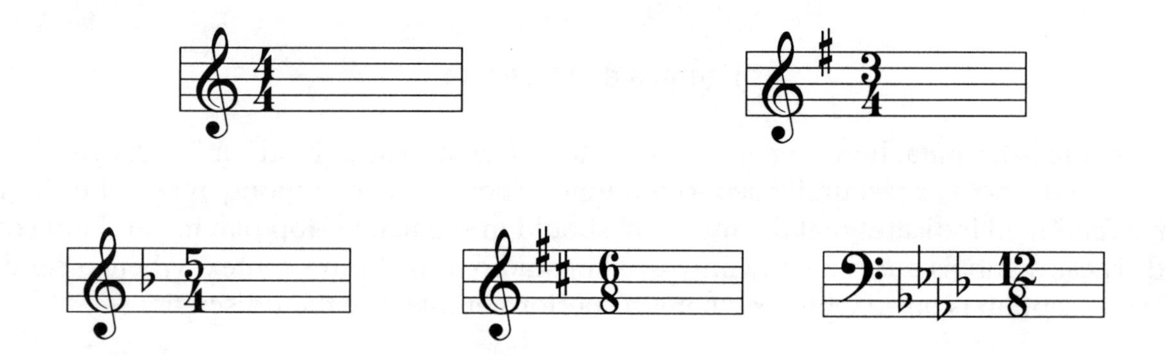

The most common time signature used is 4/4, and may also be referred to as common time. A "C" may be used in place of 4/4.

Do not confuse common time with cut time. Cut time, or *alla breve, refers to cutting the time value in half. This is indicated by a common time sign with a line drawn through the middle.

**Alla breve - (AH-la BRAY-vay) A tempo mark indicated by the sign ₵, for quick double time, with the half note rather than the quarter note as the beat. In other words, 2/2 instead of 4/4.*

MUSICAL MARKINGS & READING TIPS

Reading Tips

Reading, especially sight reading, has always been the guitarist's Achilles heel—no matter the level or genre of the guitarist. Following the suggestions below will get you on your way to becoming a literate, articulate musician.

The Tennis Match Syndrome

When reading a chart for the first time, never take your eyes off the music. Most guitarists look at the music, then look at their guitar neck. This process is generally repeated on every measure and sometimes for every beat. If you did not know better you would think they were watching a tennis match.

Especially when reading chords, it may be necessary to glance at your fingerboard occasionally. This should only be done with your *peripheral vision and never outright stare at the guitar. Your eyes should never completely leave the music.

When your eyes leave the music they have to find their way back which makes it almost impossible to read music with any degree of accuracy or consistency. This is a hard habit to break, but it is your first obstacle to overcome and possibly the most monumental.

Voiceleading

Keep your chord voicings in the same category if possible and move your hands as little as possible. If there are any common fingers used on coinciding chords do not release pressure as it will help give a legato sound and hold your place on your fingerboard.

Look Ahead

Most guitarists are only aware of the chord of the moment and do not look ahead or see the larger more over riding design of the chord progression. When a chord is for a duration of four beats, you should be setting your course of action instead of just staring at the same chord. Only look at the chord of the moment for one beat, then force your eyes to look ahead. A good reader will always have four to eight measures charted out as they are playing. I know this sounds like a huge undertaking, but it is like any other craft—if you take it slow and practice consistently it will not really be that difficult.

**peripheral vision = The section that is on the edge or rim of your visual spectrum.*

MUSICAL MARKINGS & READING TIPS

Reading Tips

Substitution by Elimination

If your hands and mind cannot immediately react to the chord symbol, substitute down. This is an acceptable practice among all rhythm guitar players. In fact, if I am playing the Freddie Green style, I generally only play the 3rd, 7th and Root or 5th no matter what the symbol indicates.

There are countless ways chords can be substituted down, but these are what I consider the most useful.

Example

Original Chord Symbol		Substitution Possibilities
C7♯9♭13	=	C7♯9, C7♭13, C7, C
Cm9	=	Cm7, Cm
C+7	=	C+ (the triad can never be altered)
C11	=	C7sus4
C6	=	C

Substitiution by Addition

Substitution by addition is another story and you must be very careful when you use this technique. Until you get a feel for the arrangement, other musicians etc. only play what's written or substitute by elimination.

If you would like to get a little more of a "jazz sound" the following may be what your looking for. Never use this technique when sight reading and always use sparingly.

Original Chord Symbol		Sub Possibilities
C7	=	C9, C13, C 9/13,
Cm7	=	Cm9, Cm11
C	=	C add 9, Cma7, Cma7/9, C6, C6/9

* *Note that substitution possibilities for both elimination and addition can be for any key. The key signature of C is only used for an example.*

Chapter III

MUTE STROKES

Written Muted Strokes in the Contemporary Idiom

The mute or muffled stroke is notated with an X. To achieve this articulation lightly cover your strings with the left hand so there is no tonality and a muted percussive sound is attained.

Muted strokes add a nice percussive quality to a piece of music and also is an excellent technique to lock the time into the "pocket". This technique is particularly effective in contemporary idioms and in theater "pit" orchestras.

Utility voicings are very good for this technique because most of the strings have a finger on them and by just releasing pressure, the muted strum is achieved.

The examples in this chapter have the rhythm part as it would appear with *slash mark rhythm (written). They are later repeated with the fingering, TAB and picking indications (sounds). Get the sound in your head. Experiment with other chord shapes and picking—none of this is written in stone!

Contemporary Rhythms #1

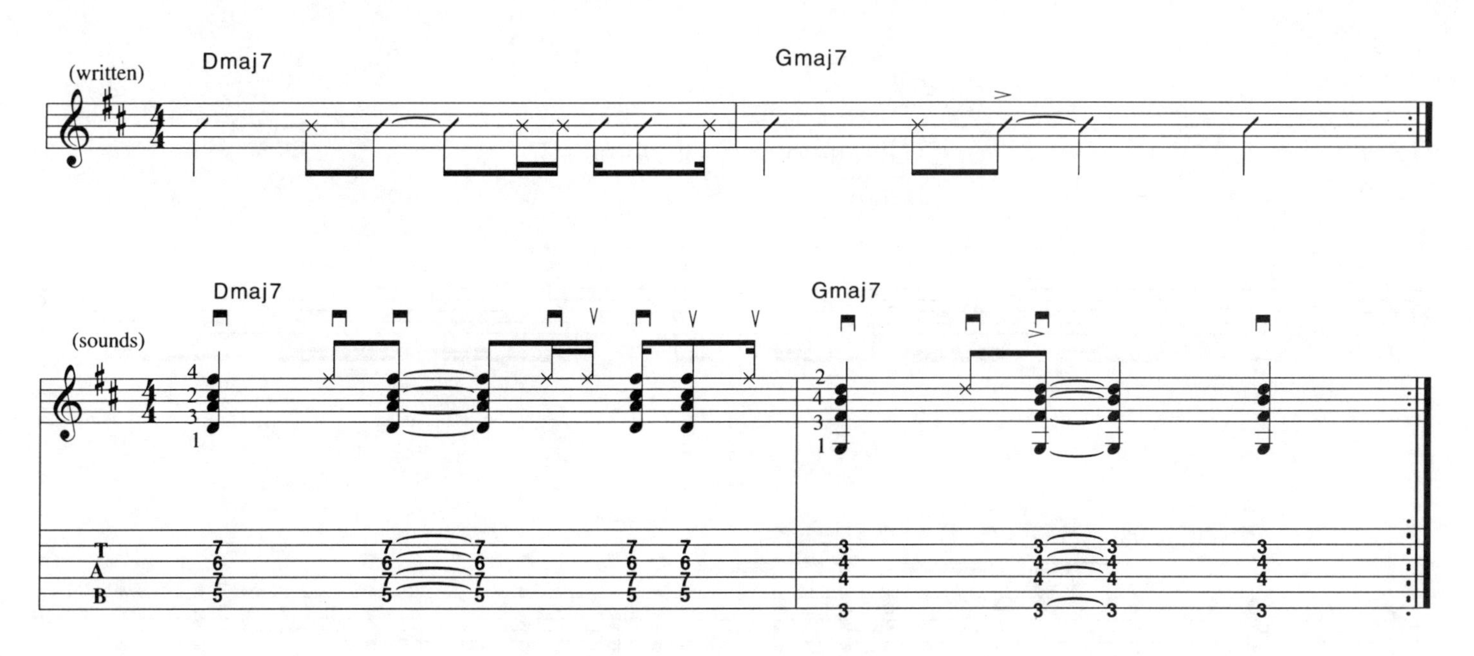

Slash marks are diagonal lines going between the second and fourth lines of the staff indicating the rhythm, but leaving the exact chord voicings to the guitarist.

MUTE STROKES

Contempory Rhythm—con't

Contemporary Rhythms #2

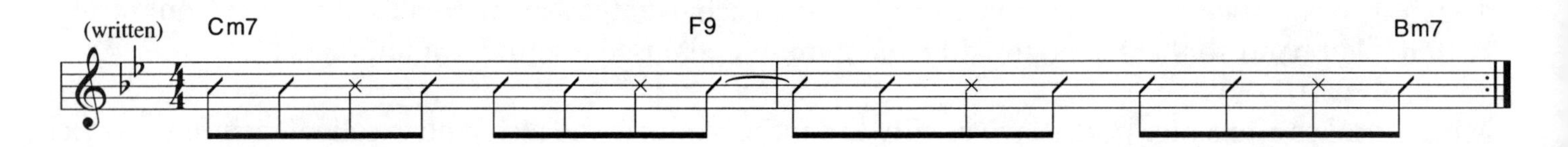

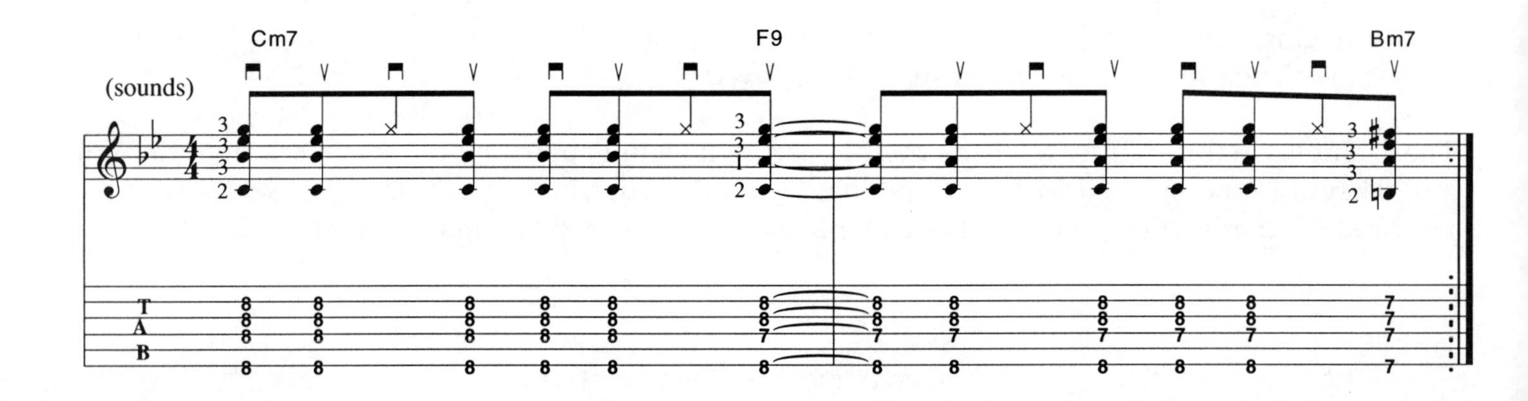

Contemporary Rhythms #3

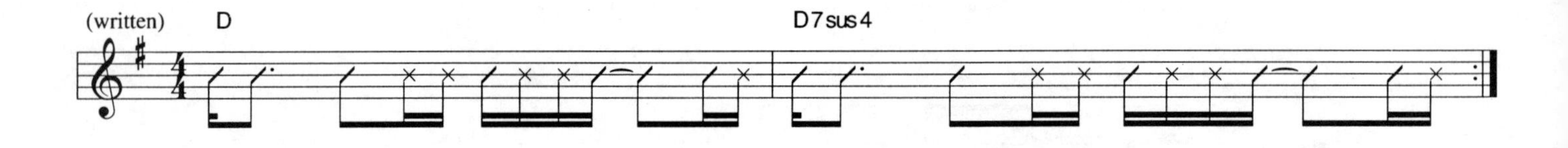

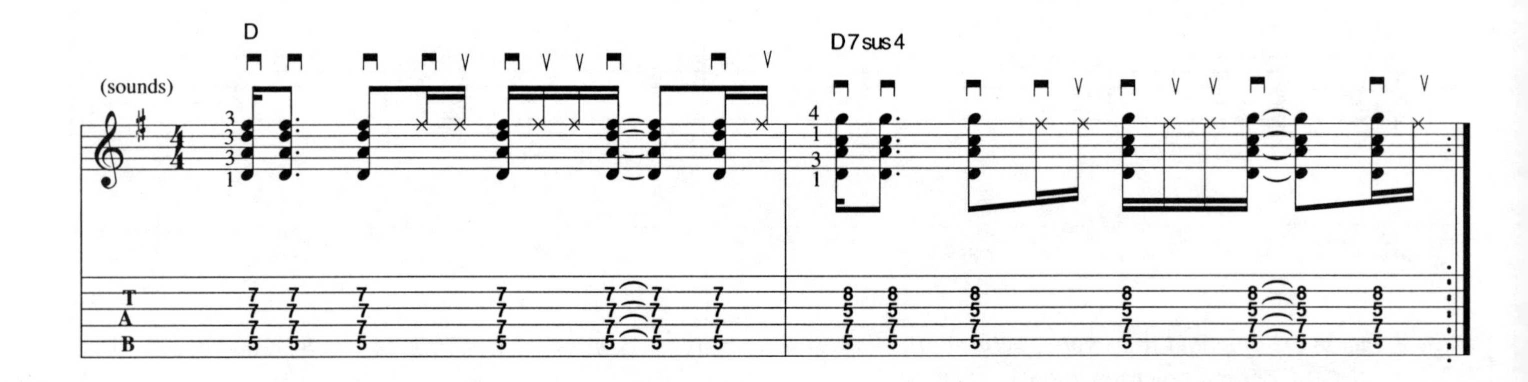

MUTE STROKES

Contempory Rhythm—con't

Example #4

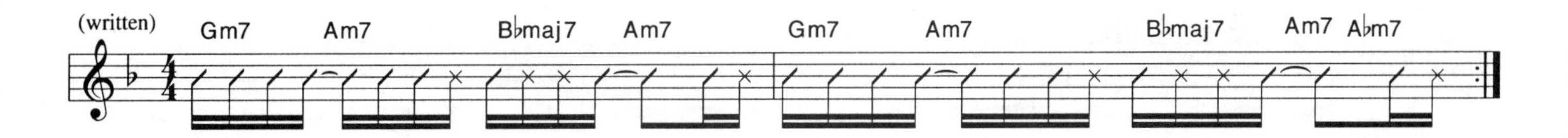

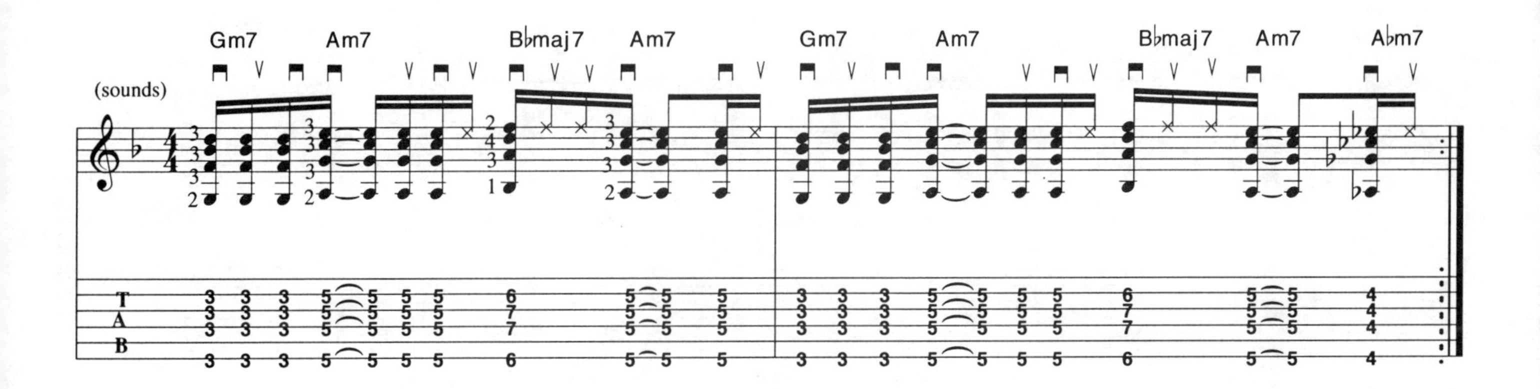

Example #5

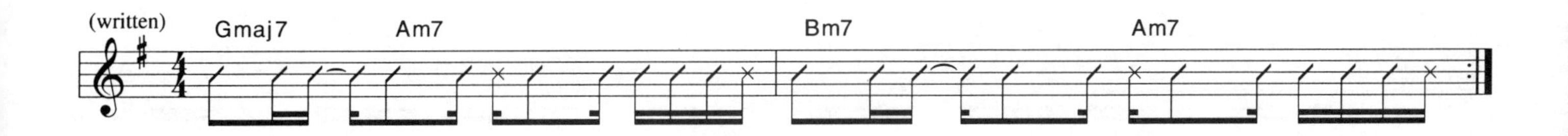

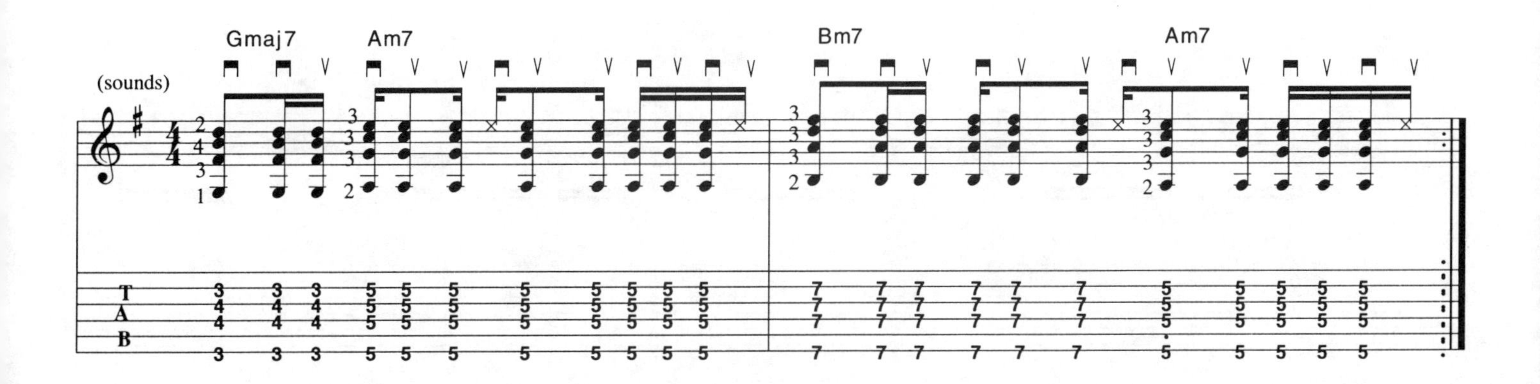

MUTE STROKES

Contempory Rhythm—con't

Example #6

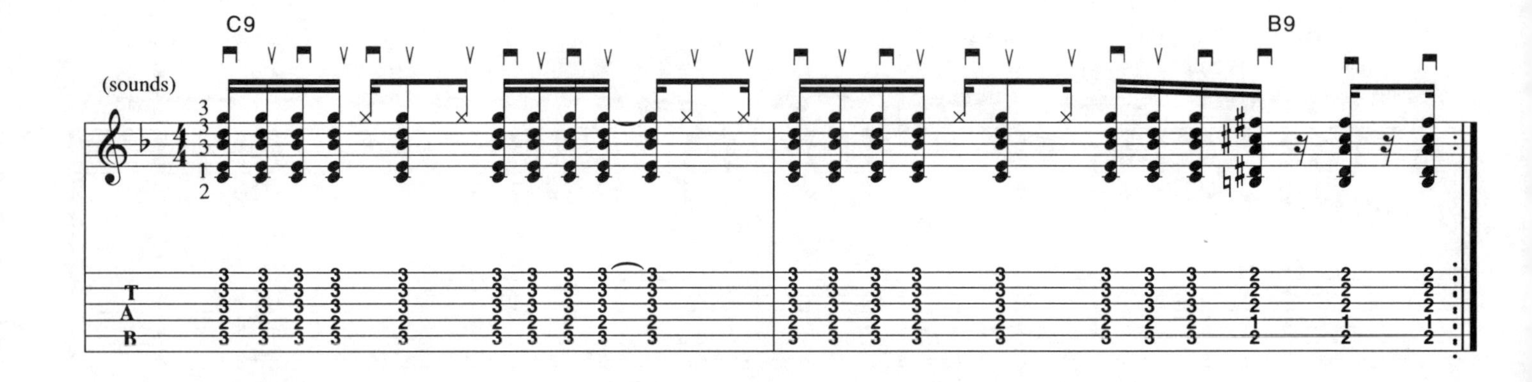

Example #7

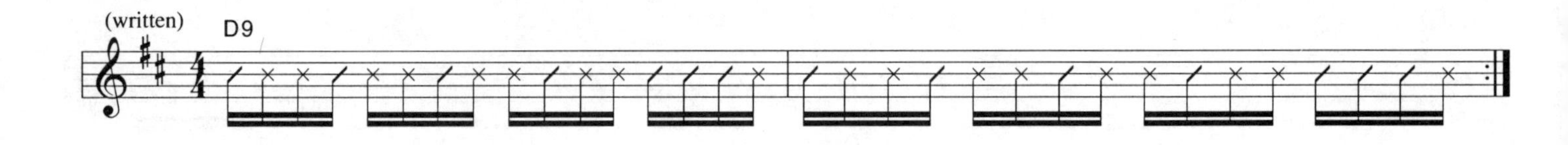

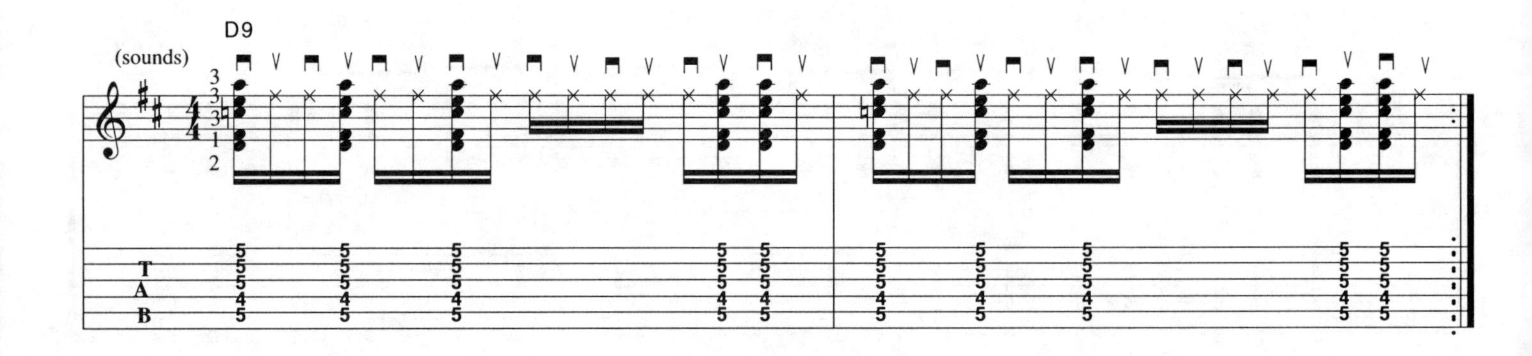

MUTE STROKES

Assumed Mute Stroke

The assumed mute stroke is more of a stylistic idiosyncrasy than a necessity. When a rest is written, the rhythm guitarist can substitute the muted sound in place of absolute silence. This helps keep the time and often adds that little something that puts the rhythm in the *pocket. The problem is knowing when and where to use this technique. The best way to learn is to listen to rhythm guitarists and be aware of what they are doing.

An excellent way to develop a feel for the assumed mute stroke is to work out the rhythm guitar parts from theater productions. These are generally referred to as pit bands and accompany traditional Broadway style shows. Similar rhythms are often noted in *dance band arrangements as well.

Musicians often make fun of this style calling it corny, but the truth is few guitarists really have the ability to execute the part with the proper feel and voicings. Pit orchestra gigs are one of the most lucrative and secure positions a guitarists can acquire. Putting all this aside, theater rhythm guitar, is one of the best ways to develop independence of both right and left-hands. The technical facility of this style can be transferred to any other style you perform in.

The orchestral rhythms notated are what I consider common. Any guitarist attempting to get a job in this genre should be aware of these styles. There is quite a bit of controversy over the way these should be executed and there is no one correct way. The manner in which I will illustrate these concepts was shown to me by one of the best rhythm guitarists I ever heard, William G. Leavitt. Bill was considered, by anyone who ever heard him, the consummate rhythm guitar player. He stopped actively performing in the early 1970's to devote his time to writing and setting up the guitar program at Berklee College. Until his untimely death twenty years later he was still sought after for his great rhythm guitar sound.

The following is the suggested chord forms for the orchestral rhythm examples:

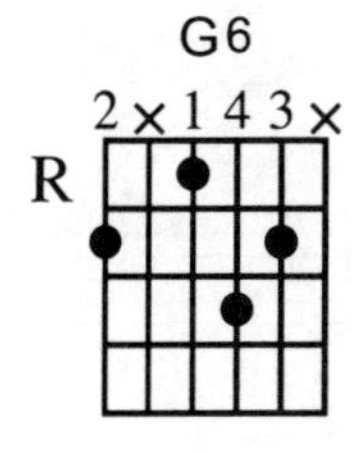

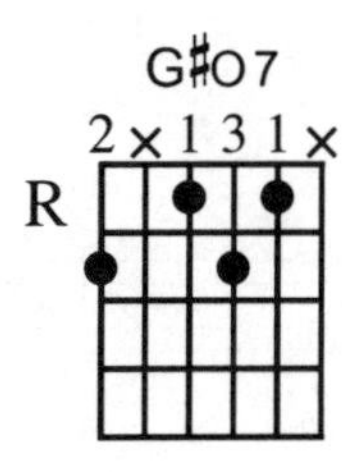

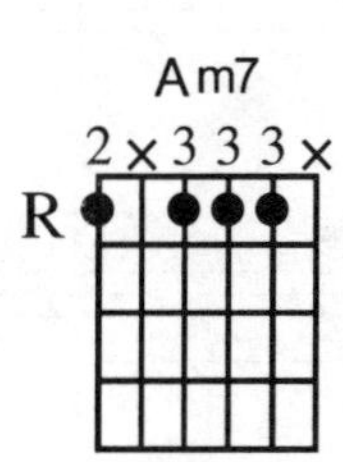

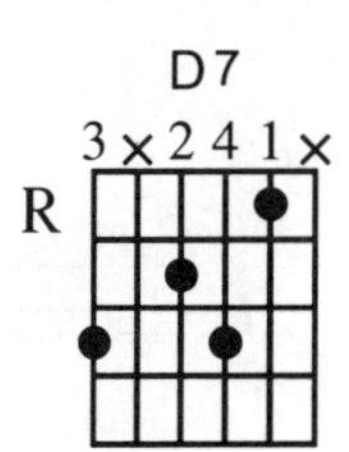

* *Dance Bands = Also referred to as big bands. This usually is a 15 to 17 piece ensemble playing dance music made popular in the 1940's and 50's.*

* *Pocket = A term used, especially among the rhythm section, to indicate that the perfect feel and groove has been achieved.*

Assumed Mute Stroke—con't

As with contemporary rhythms, these orchestral examples are presented in the manner the music is actually written and the way it should sound. Note that tapping is also indicated. This refers to tapping your foot. It is imperative that you tap your foot to keep the time and groove. Classical musicians will disagree with me, but the test is how well you can execute the part. This technique is what works for me and 99% of everyone I've shown it to.

Orchestral 2 Beat

Tap on 1 & 3:

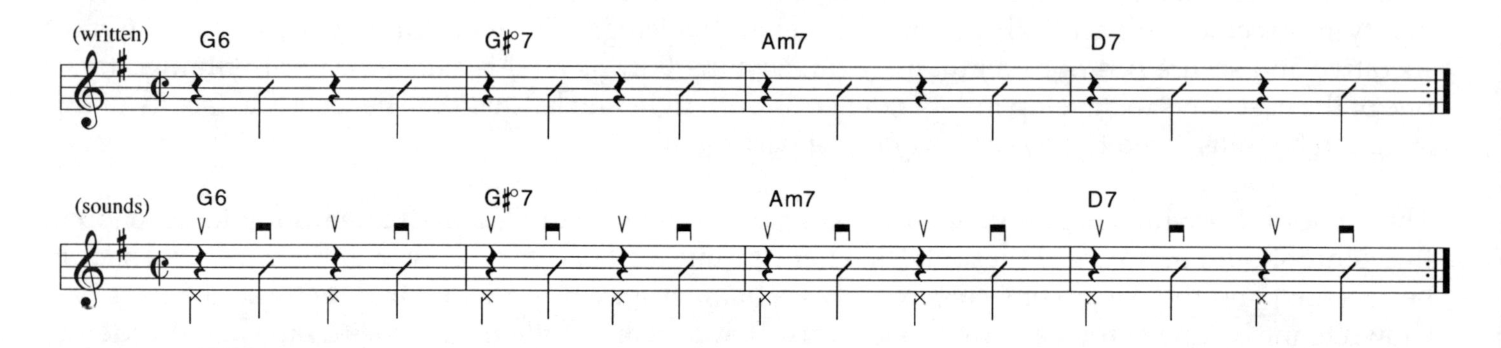

Note that this and the following examples are in *cut time.

Orchestral 2 Beat Going Into Fast 4

Tap on 1 & 3 throughtout:

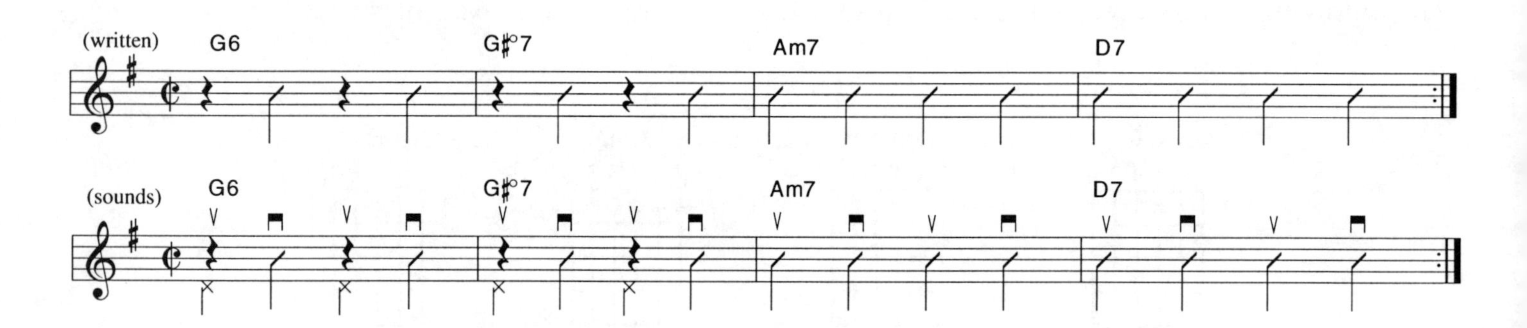

Cut time = A tempo mark indicated by a common time signature with a line through it. It replaces the half note rather than the quarter note as the beat. In other words, 2/2 instead of 4/4.

MUTE STROKES

Assumed Mute Stroke—con't

Orchestral Swing Waltz

Tap in 3:

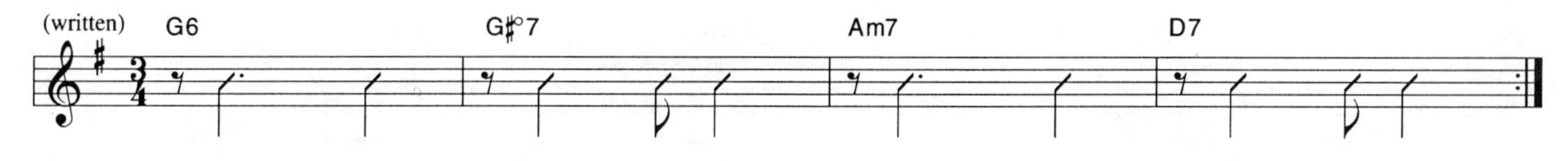

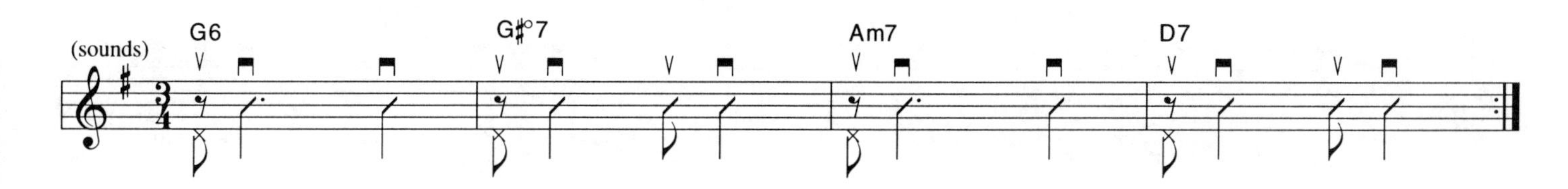

Orchestral Shuffle

Tap in 4:

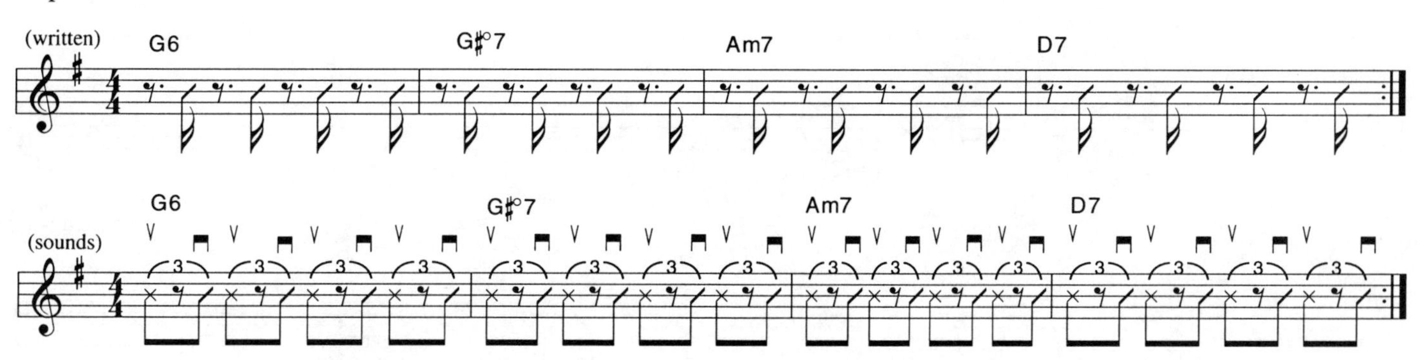

Orchestral Beguine

Tap in 4:

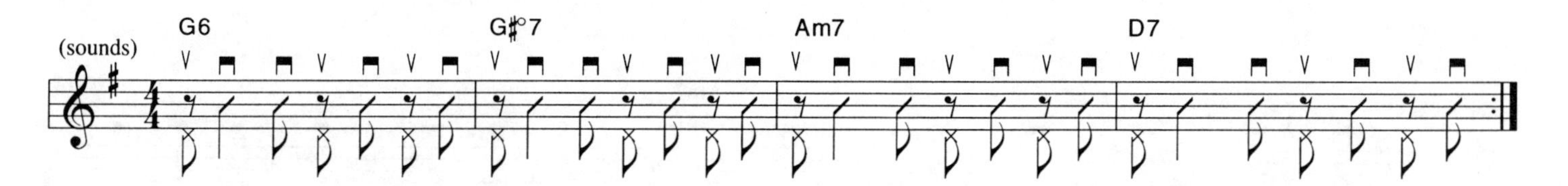

MUTE STROKES

Assumed Mute Stroke—con't

Orchestral Rumba

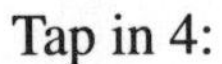

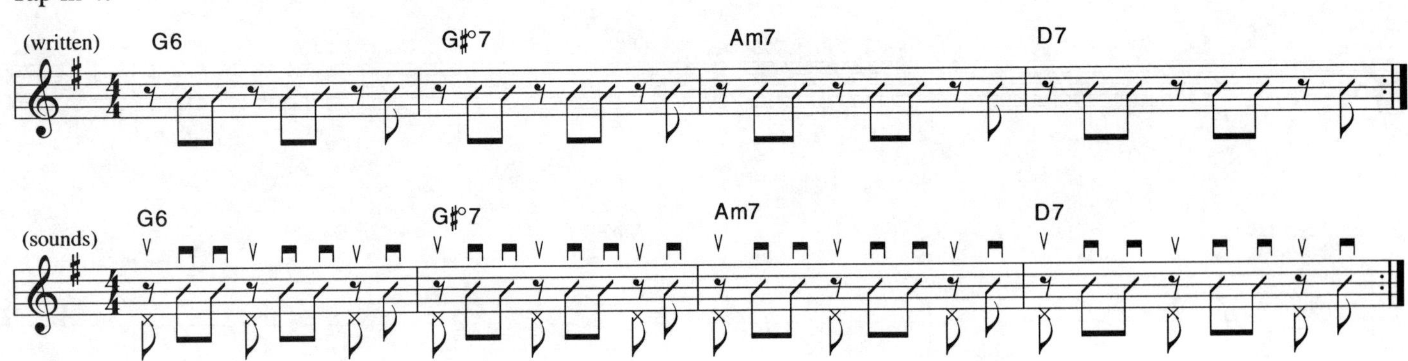

Orchestral Bossa

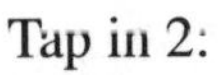

Orchestral 5/4

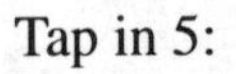

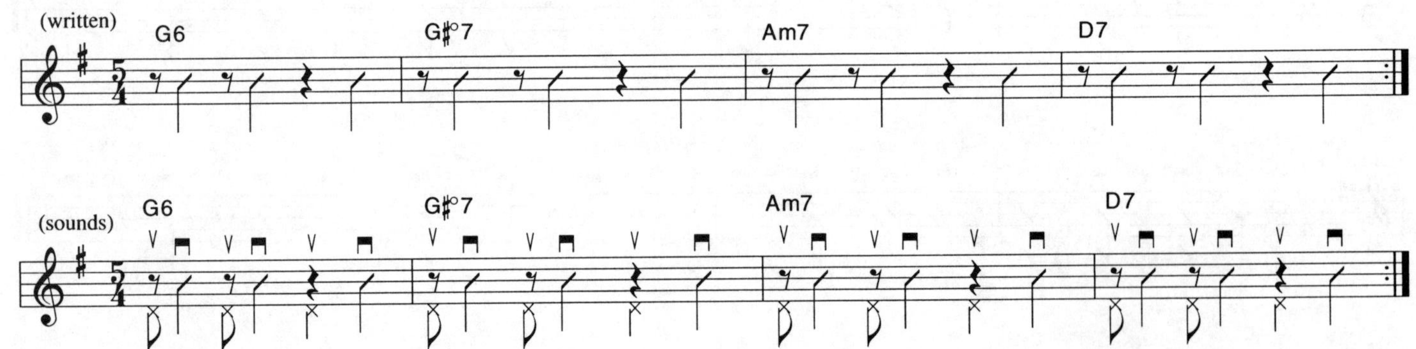

Chapter IV

SMALL BAND RHYTHM GUITAR

The following "real world" examples will provide the opportunity to see a typical rhythm guitar chart. Once again, the examples are first notated as you would see them in a chart format with *slash rhythm (as written) and a second time (as played) with suggested voicings, rhythms, positions, fingerings and picking indications.

I strongly suggest that after you have learned each example, experiment with different chord voicings and picking. The ones provided have been given considerable thought so always go through them first. Pay special attention to the picking as this will set the groove and is what often separates a pro from a novice rhythm guitarist.

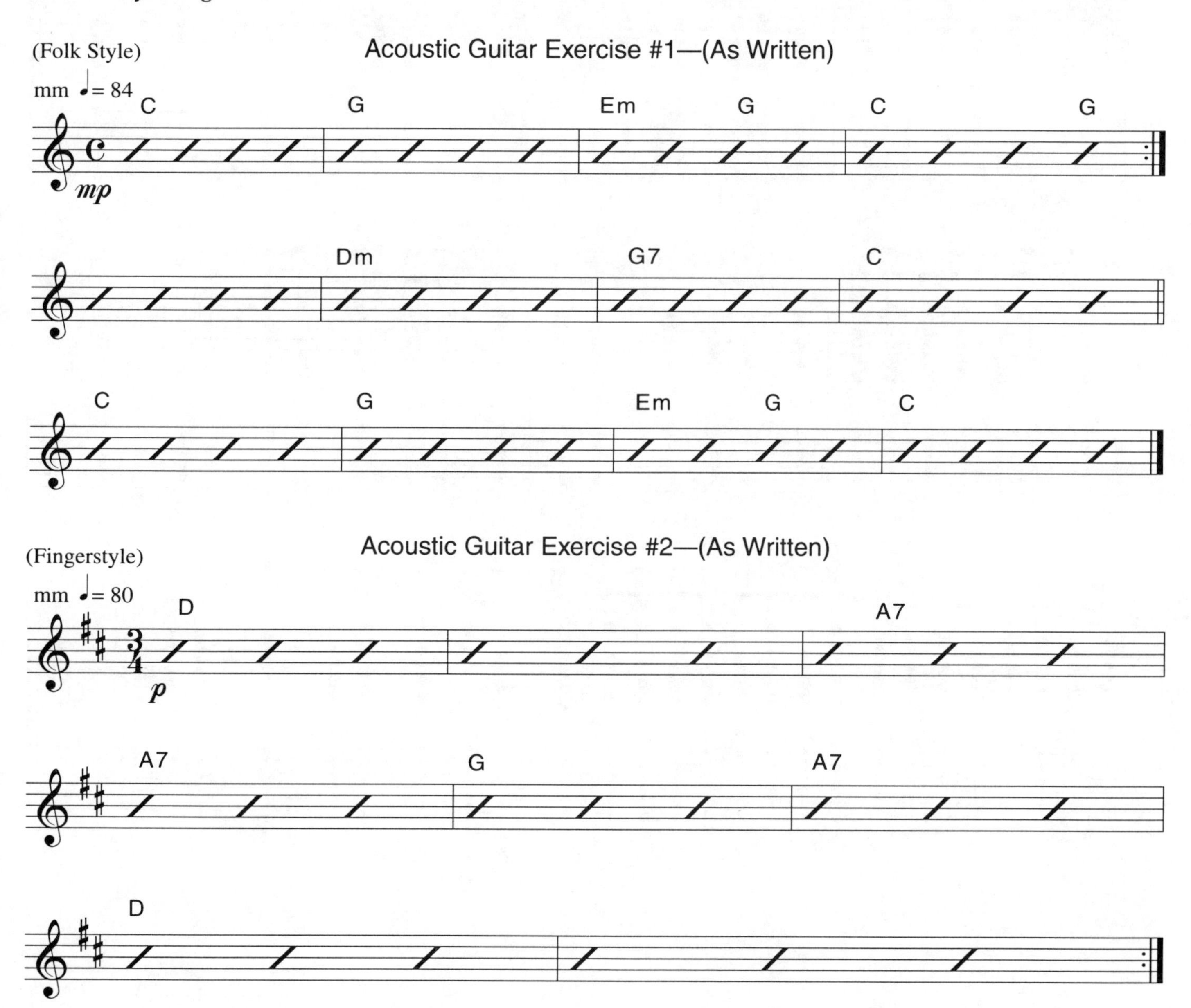

Slash marks are four thick diagonal lines going between the second and fourth lines of the staff. Slash marks indicate that the choice of rhythm is up to the individual performer.

STYLISTIC EXAMPLES

When a piece of music is written for acoustic guitar the term "folk" is often used. Something similar to the exercise below is generally called for:

Acoustic Guitar Exercise #1—(As Played)

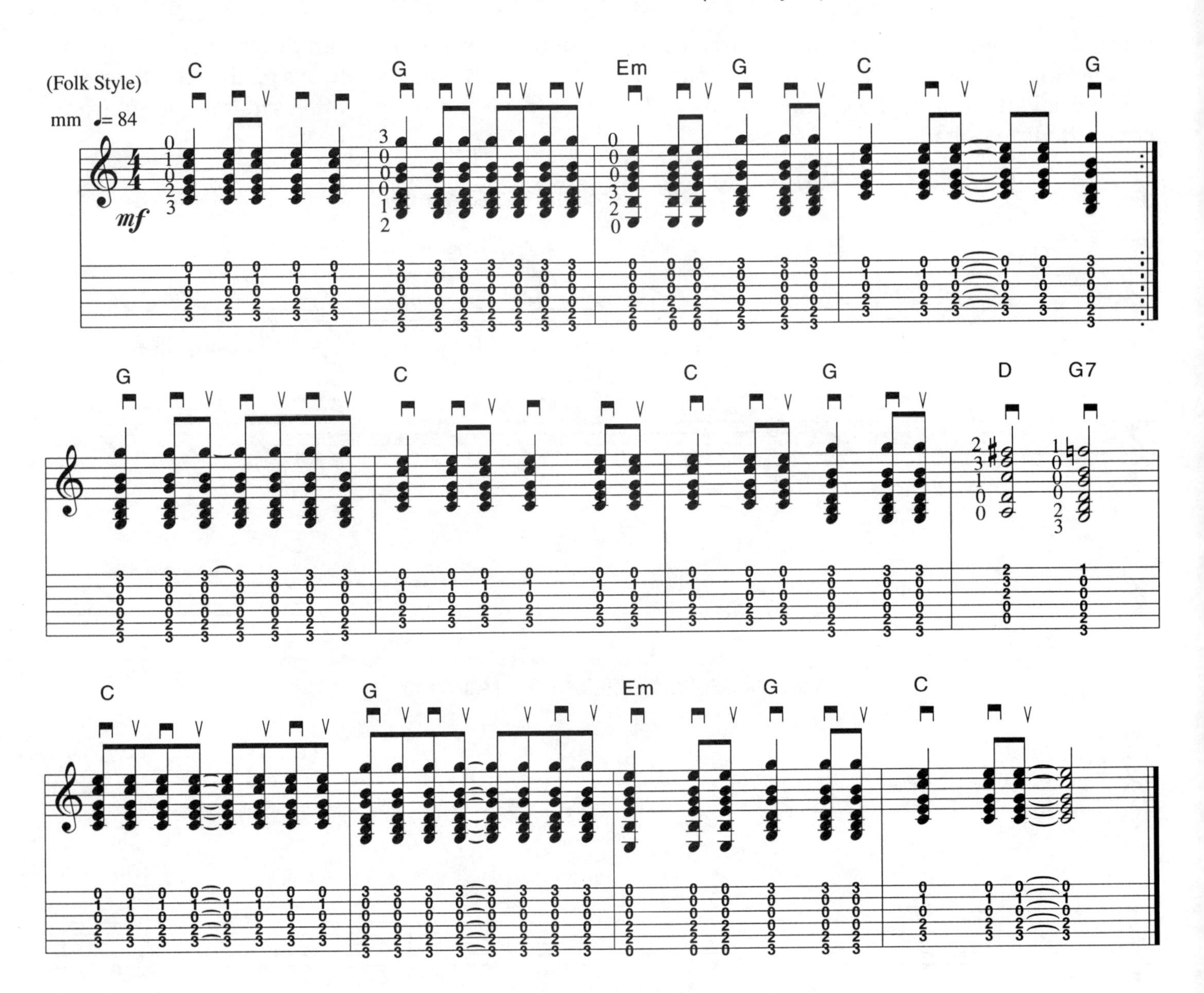

SMALL BAND RHYTHM GUITAR

The term "finger picking" (or fingerstyle) generally does not necessarily designate you must use the fingers of your right hand. It merely designates the performer to execute the music in an arpeggio fashion similar to what is shown below. The "Acoustic Guitar Exercise #2" is notated to be played with a pick, but experiment playing with right-hand fingers and choose what feels and sounds the best to your ear.

Acoustic Guitar Exercise #2—(As Played)

SMALL BAND RHYTHM GUITAR

Note the four to the bar slash rhythm. In a small band situation it means to "comp" as mentioned on page 31.

Small Band Blues—(As Written)

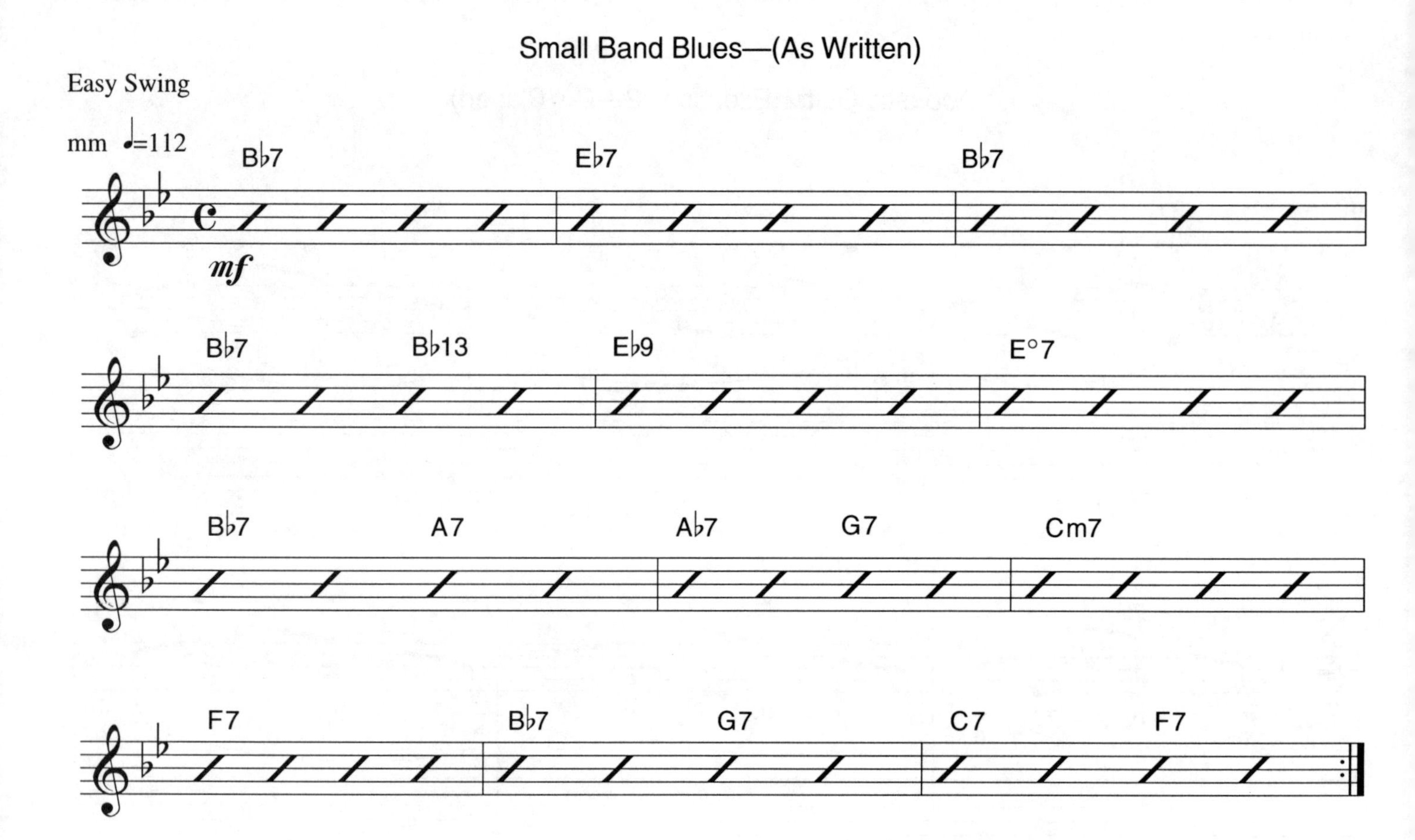

SMALL BAND RHYTHM GUITAR

Small Band Blues—(As Played)

SMALL BAND RHYTHM GUITAR

Small Band Standard Tune—(As Written)

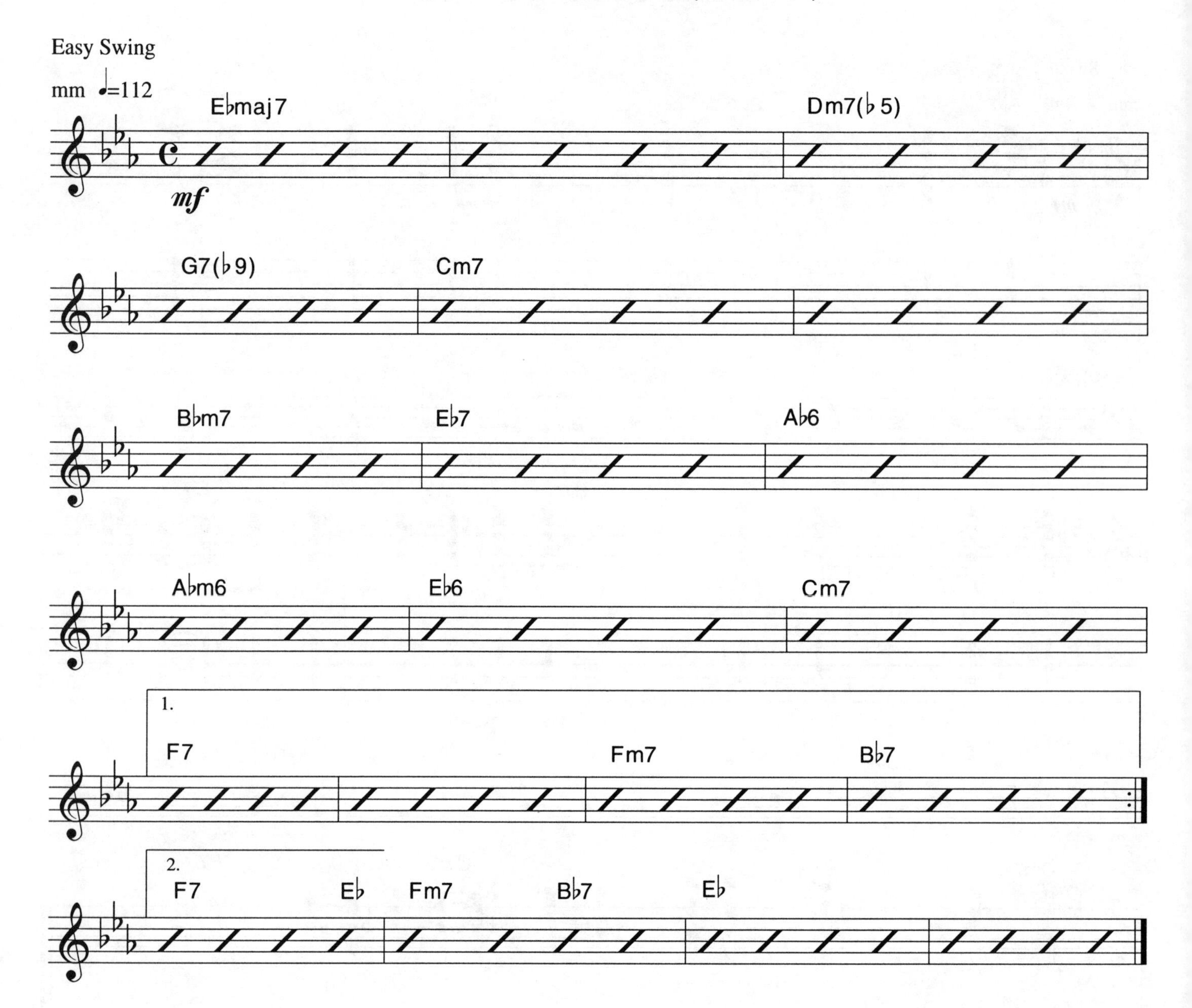

SMALL BAND RHYTHM GUITAR

Basic Latin (As Written)

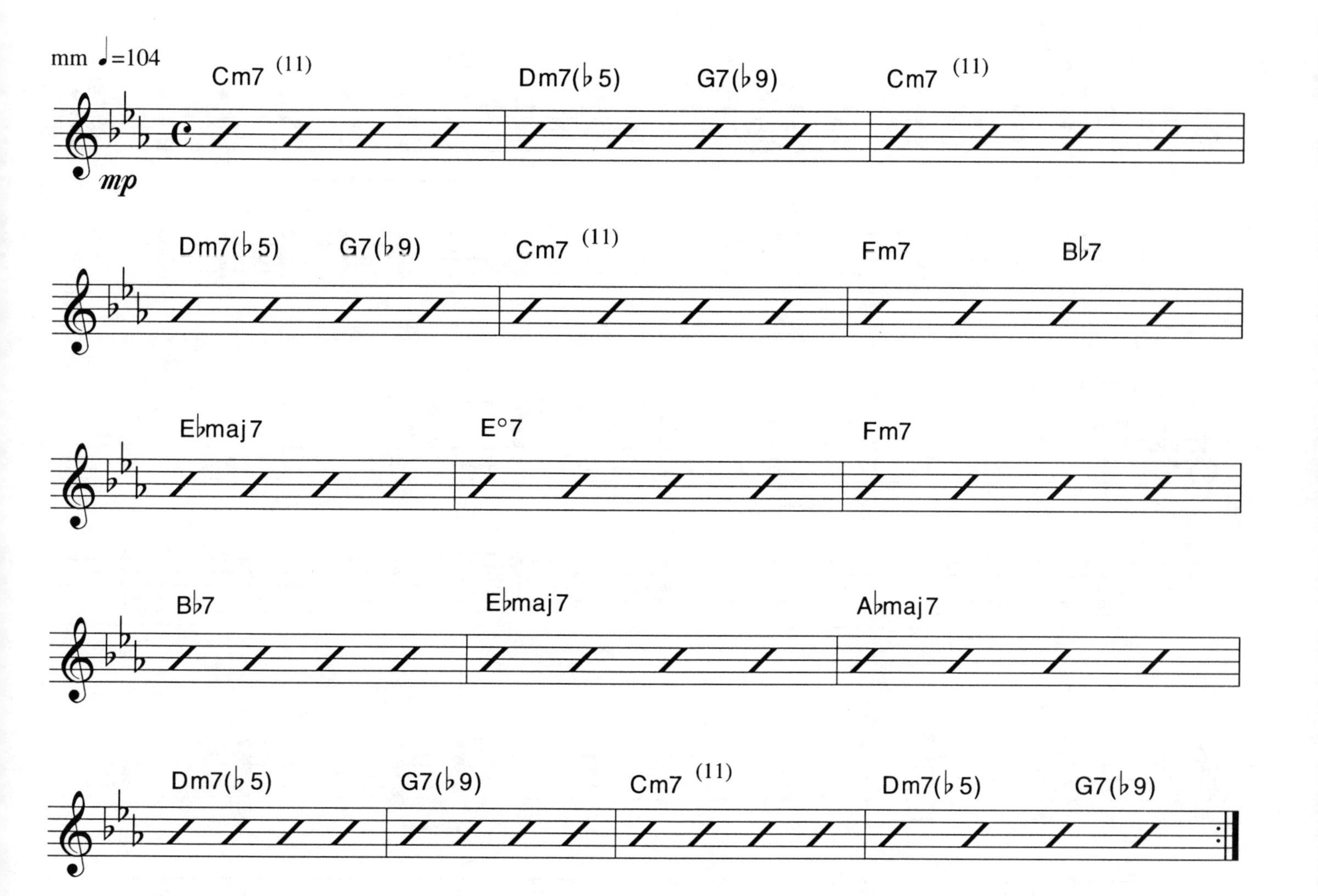

SMALL BAND RHYTHM GUITAR

Small Band Standard Tune—(As Played)

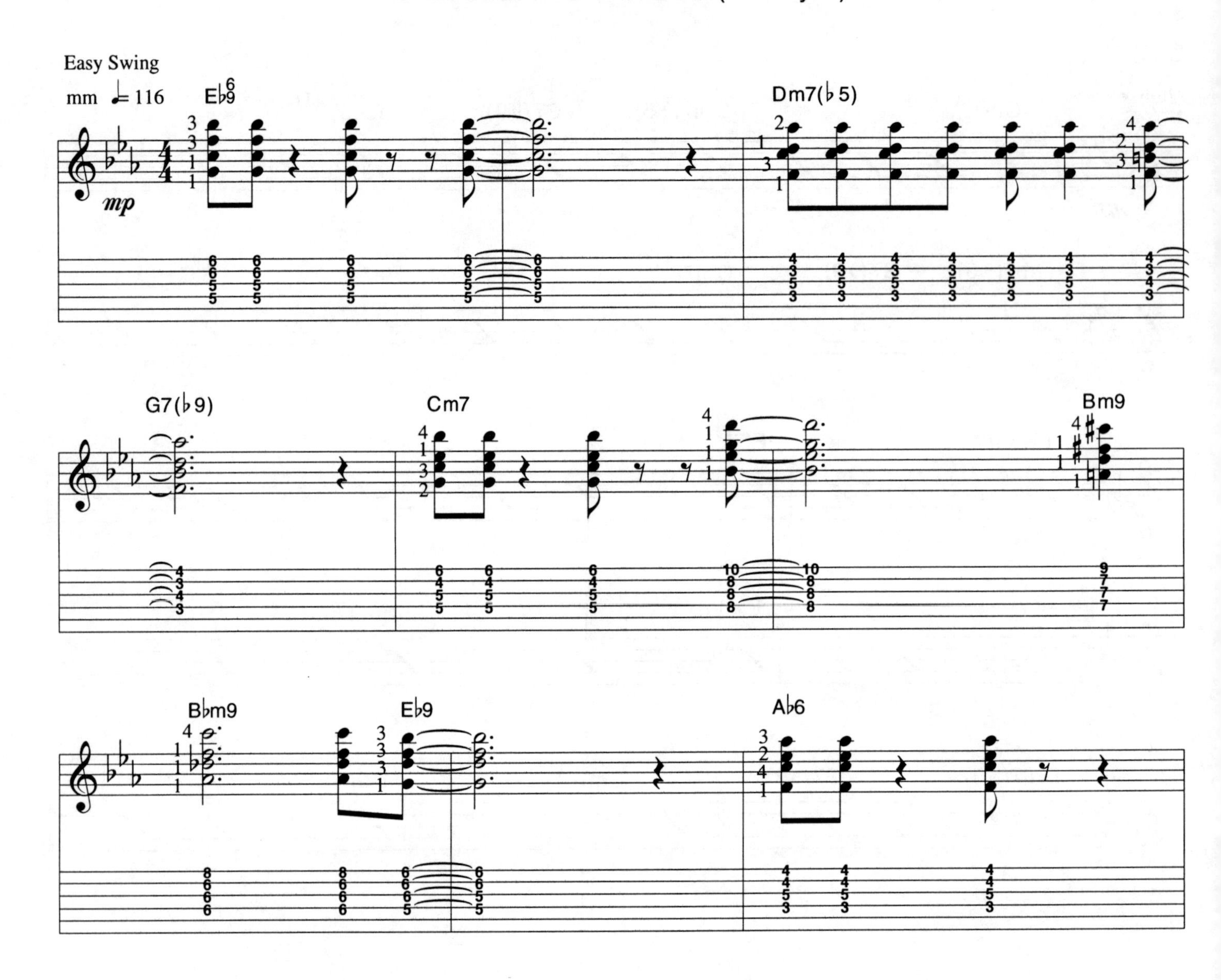

Because these chord voicings are all four parts, it makes it convenient to play with the fingers of your right-hand instead of a pick. For small band comping, it will often blend better to play with the right-hand fingers than with a pick.

SMALL BAND RHYTHM GUITAR

Small Band Standard Tune con't—(As Played)

After you feel comfortable with these voicings and rhythms, experiment on your own and try to play something similar, but possibly more applicable to your own style.

SMALL BAND RHYTHM GUITAR

Basic Latin (As Played)

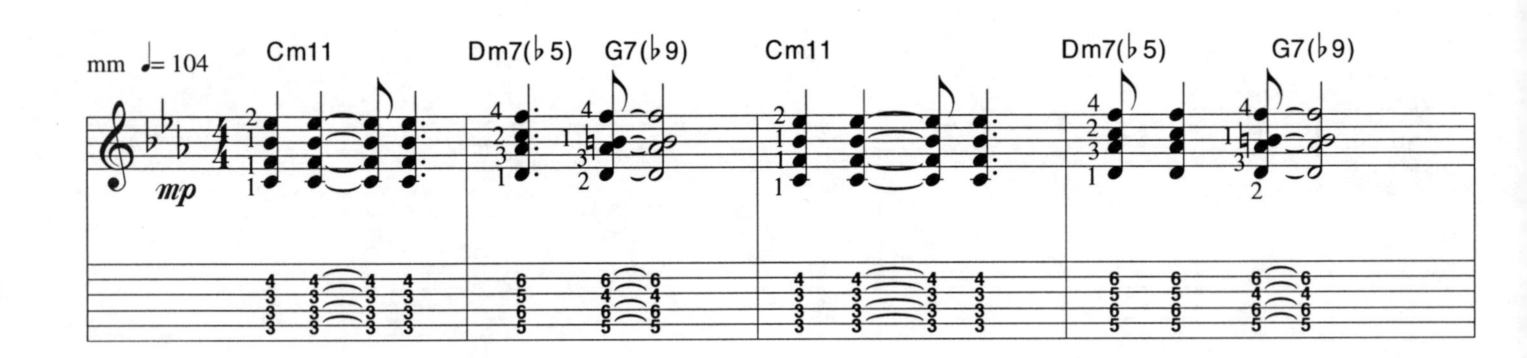

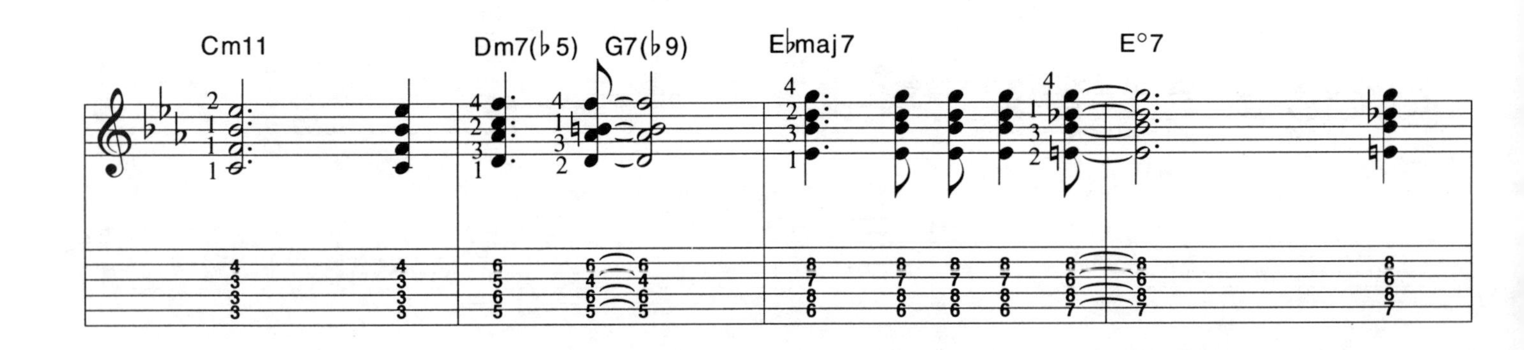

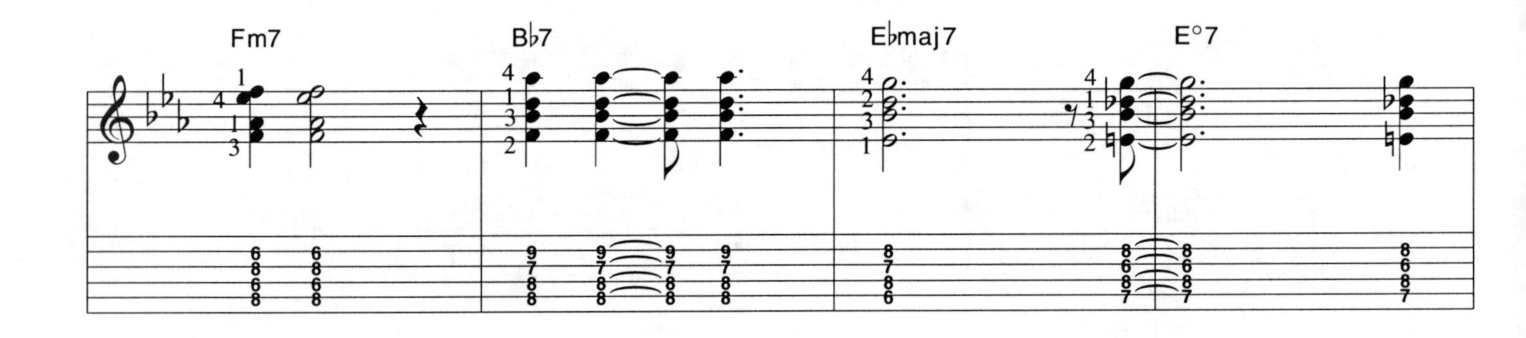

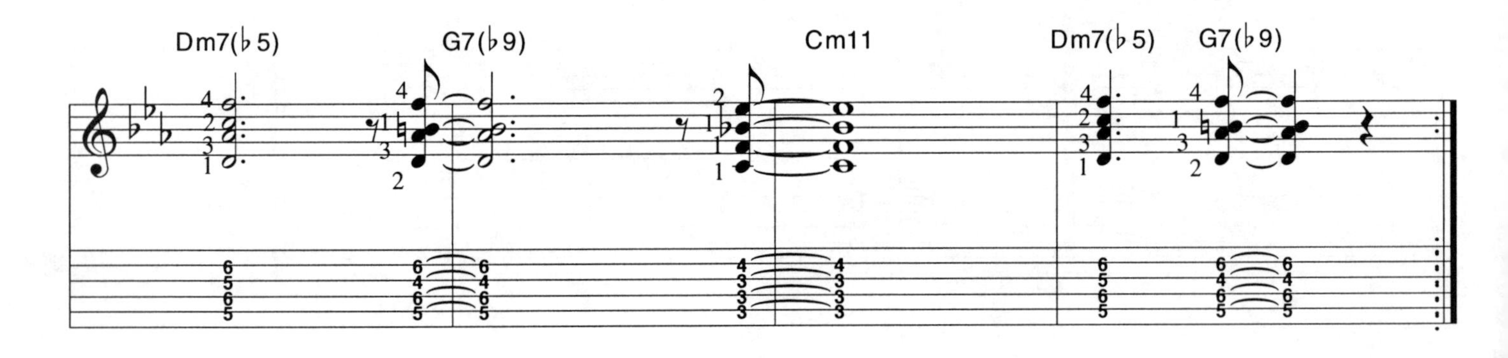

SMALL BAND RHYTHM GUITAR

Reggae (As Written)

SMALL BAND RHYTHM GUITAR

Reggae con't (As Played)

SMALL BAND RHYTHM GUITAR

Contemporary Ballad (As Written)

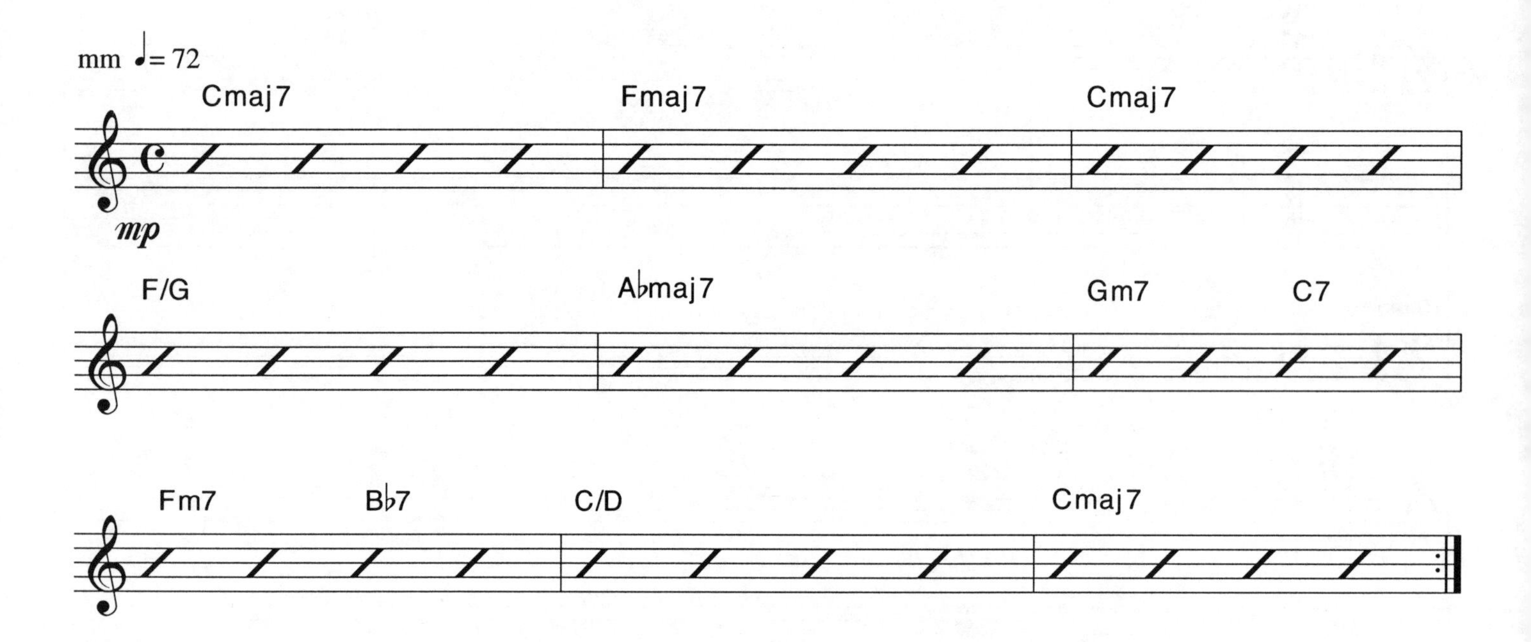

In most cases, the example above is what you will see. In theater and studio performance you may see something similar to the example below. Either way, it is imperative that you use your ears to get into the pocket and play voicings and rhythms that you feel are appropriate for the situation.

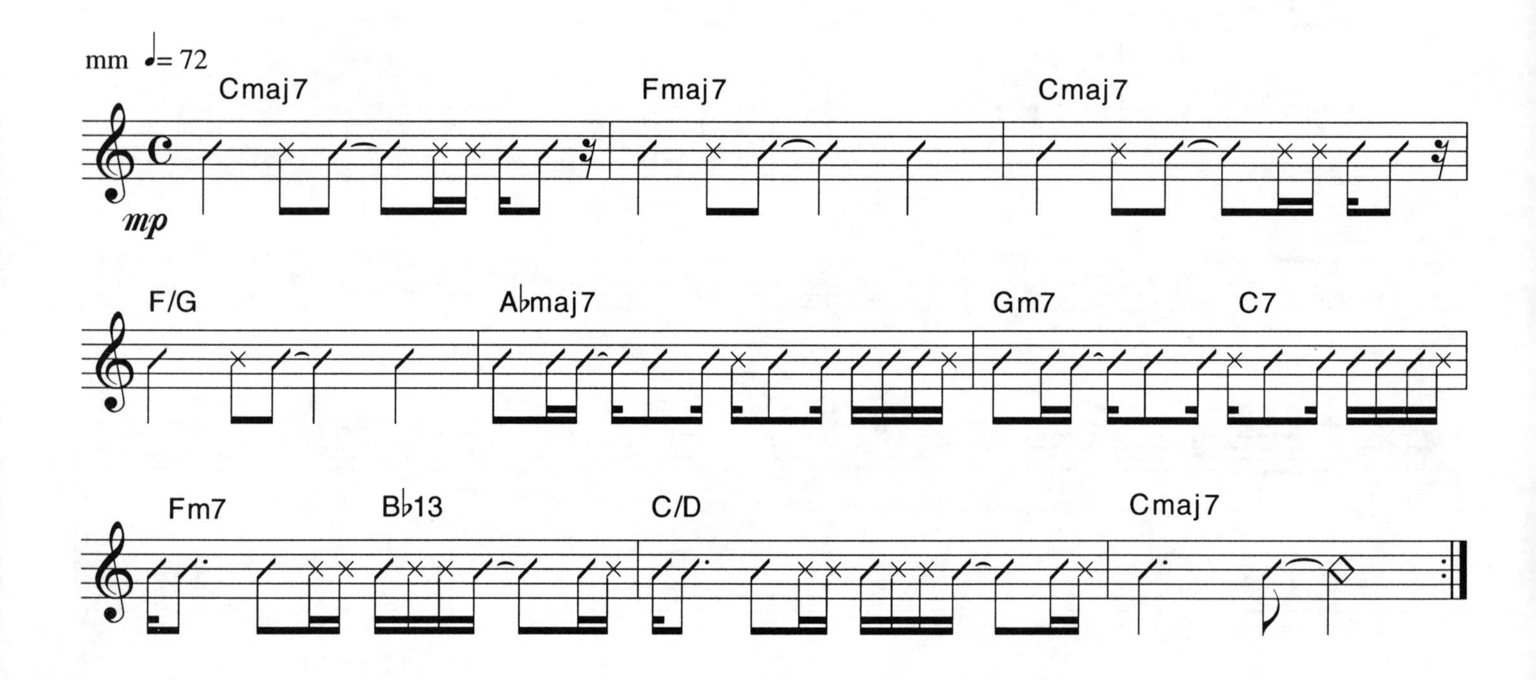

SMALL BAND RHYTHM GUITAR

Contemporary Ballad (As Played)

SMALL BAND RHYTHM GUITAR

Light Funk (As Written)

SMALL BAND RHYTHM GUITAR

50's Rock Ballad (As Written)

SMALL BAND RHYTHM GUITAR

Light Funk (As Played)

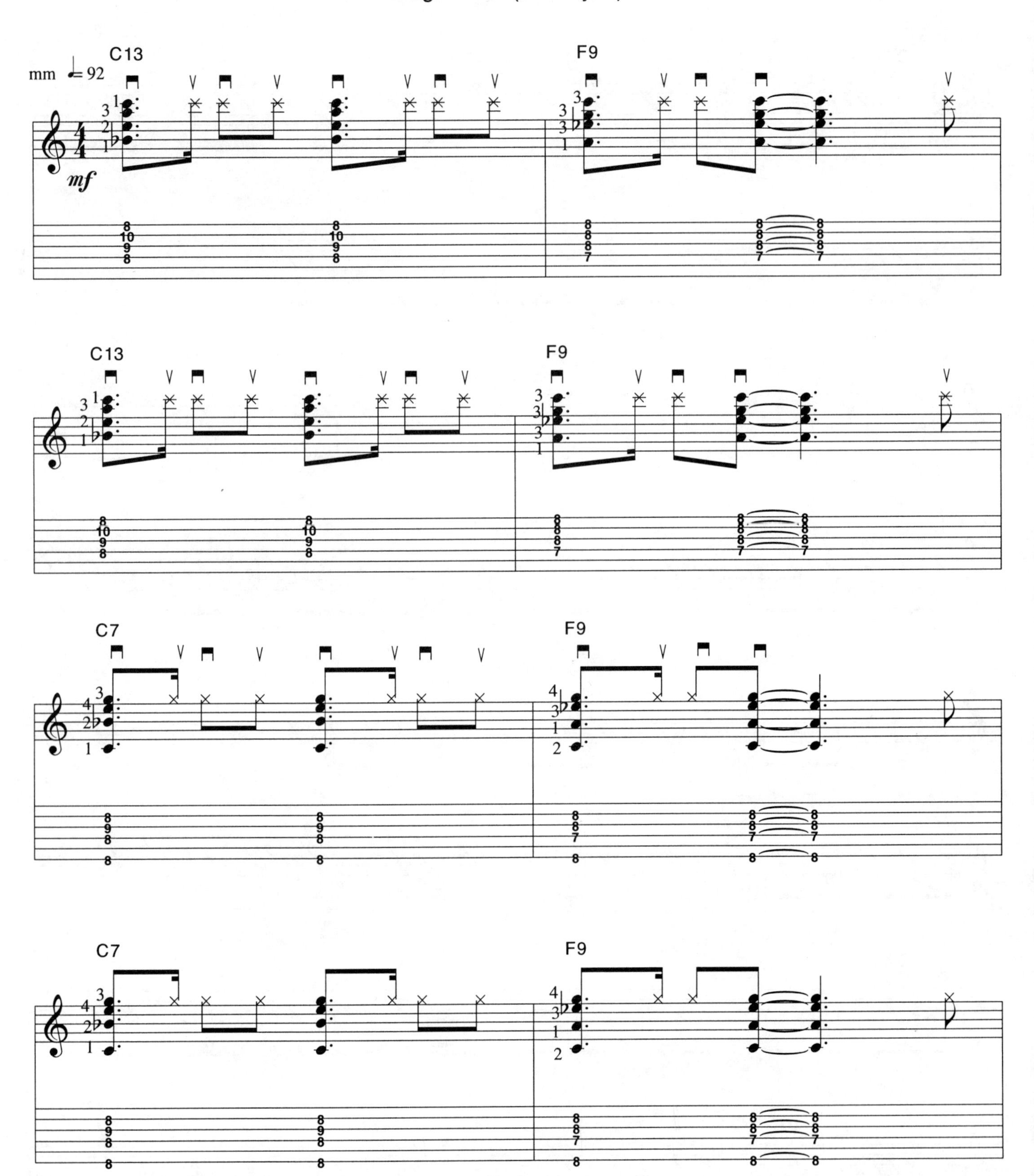

SMALL BAND RHYTHM GUITAR

Light Funk con't (As Played)

SMALL BAND RHYTHM GUITAR

50's Rock Ballad (As Played)

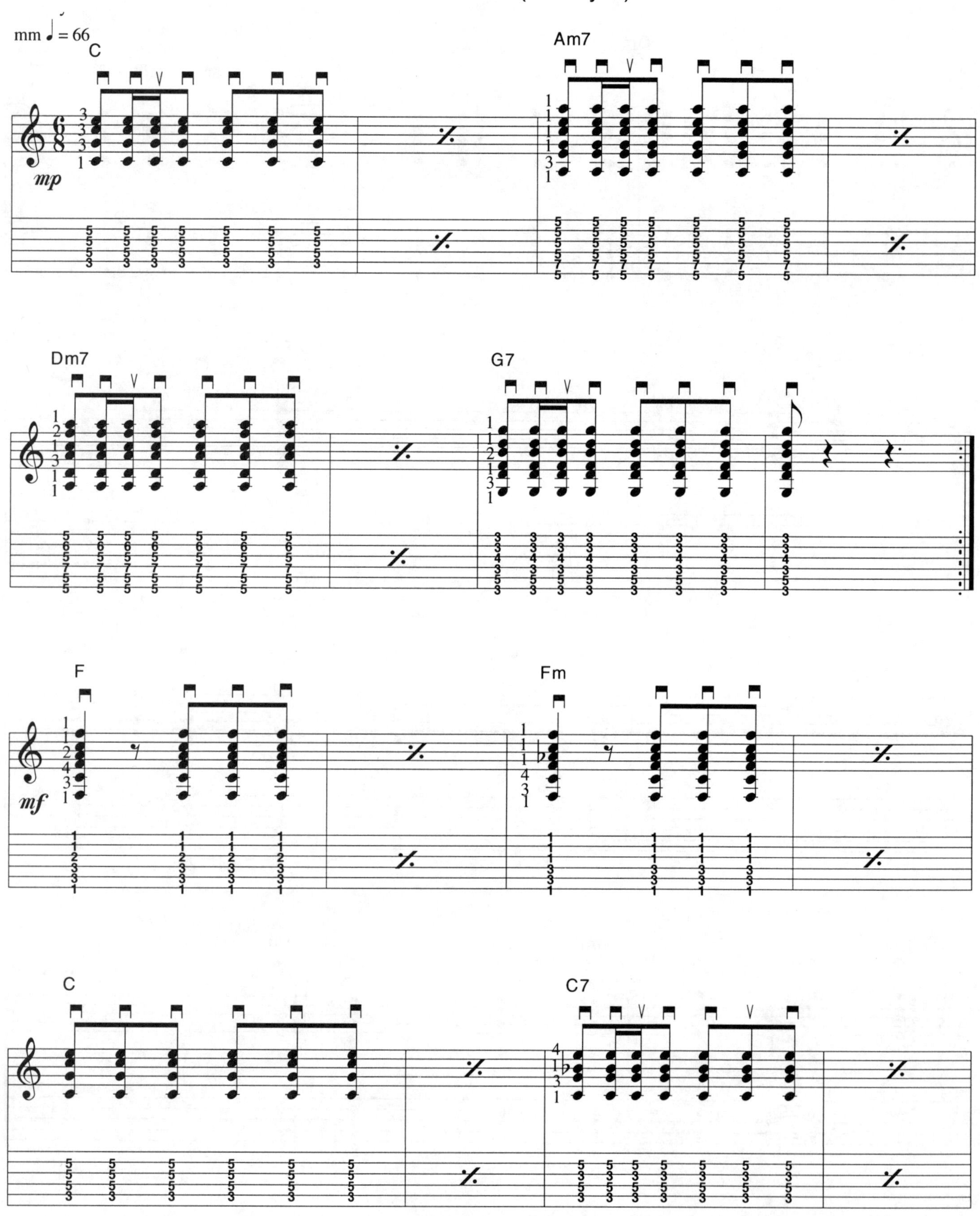

SMALL BAND RHYTHM GUITAR

50's Rock Ballad con't (As Played)

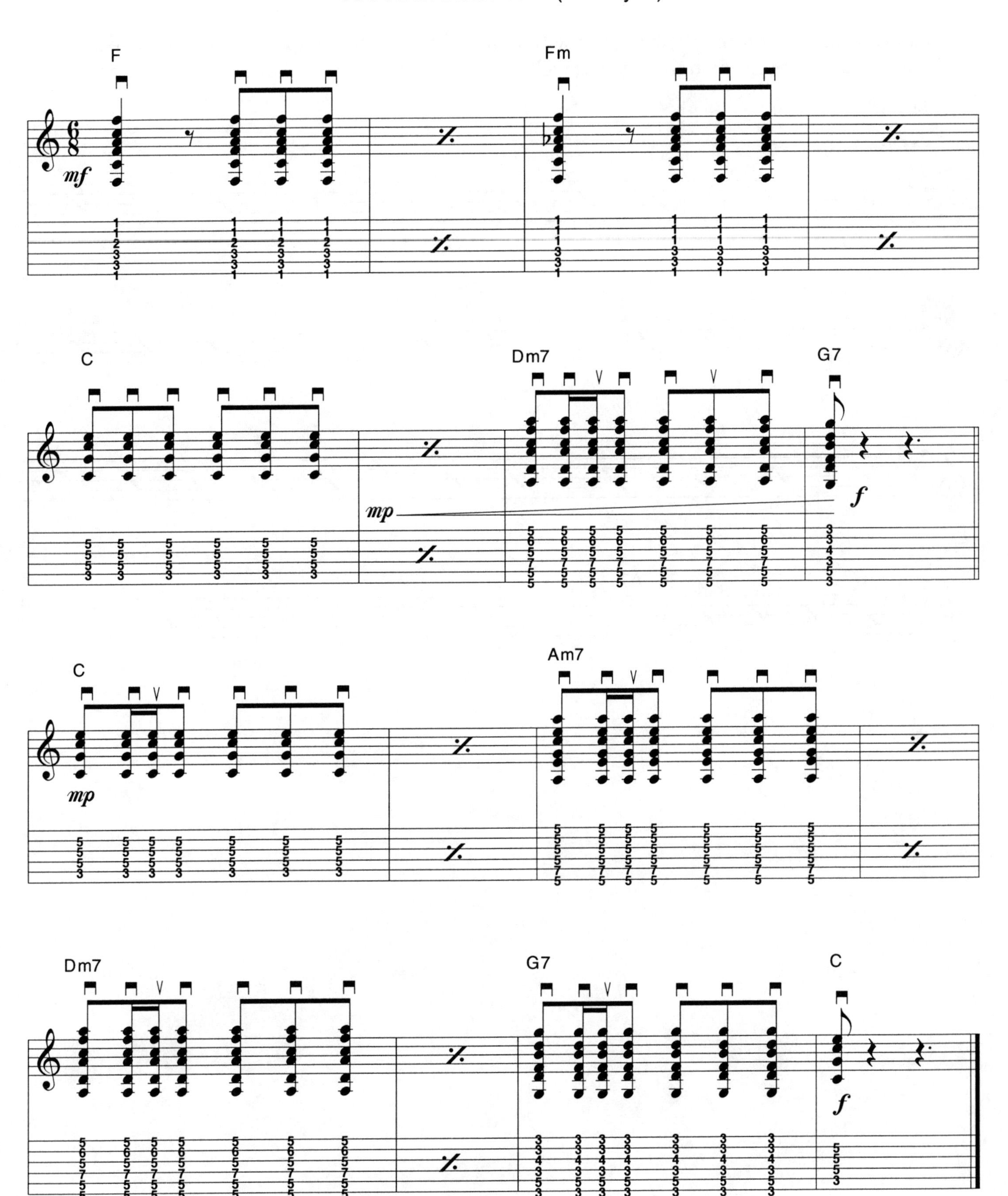

SMALL BAND RHYTHM GUITAR

Rockabilly Shuffle (As Written)

Rockabilly Shuffle is a form of swing, but with a modern more contemporary groove. Many country and western artists perform in this style as well as contemporary rock guitarists such as Brian Setzer.

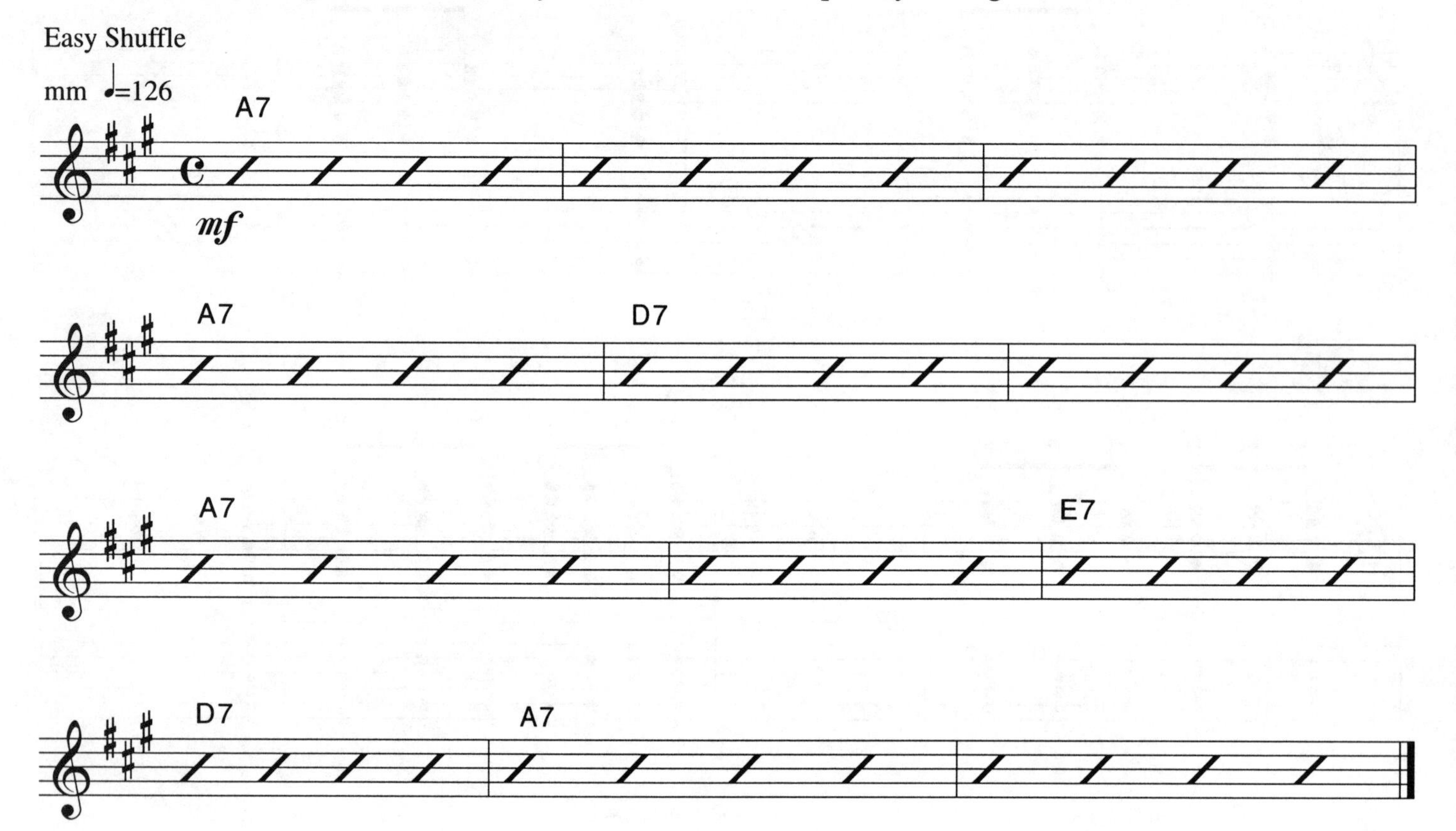

SMALL BAND RHYTHM GUITAR

Rockabilly Shuffle With Barre Chords (Played)

Full Barre chords are the most common chord family used in this style. They give a power and groove that can drive any ensemble.

SMALL BAND RHYTHM GUITAR

Rockabilly Shuffle With Power Chords (Played)

Power-chords are a family of chord voicings that use two or three notes with the most common being the root and 5th. These chords are very commonly used in the hard-rock and metal genres. By adding the 6th and flat 7 these chords now give a great groove to the rockabilly shuffle style.

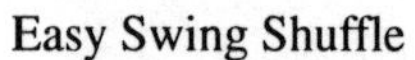

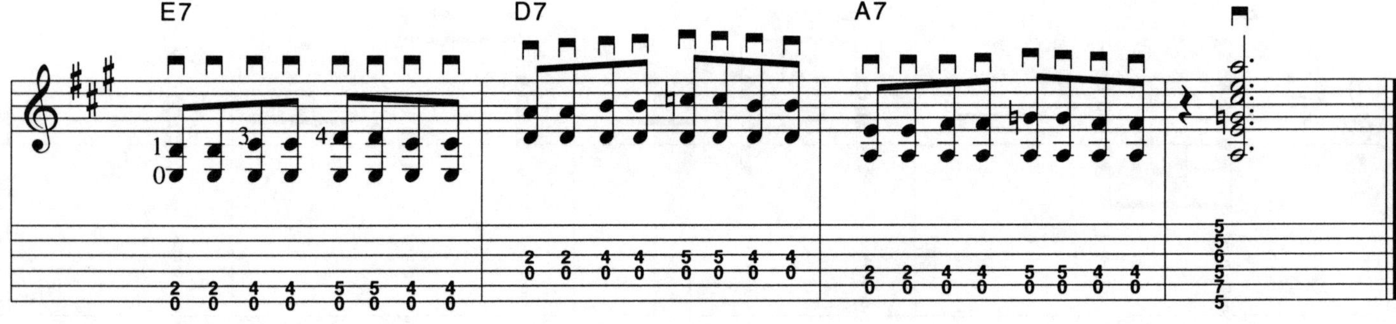

Chapter V

LARGE ENSEMBLE SWING

In this chapter, each example will be presented in three variations:

I. The first is the most basic format. The chord voicings, picking and articulations are left entirely up to the rhythm guitarist. The arranger is relying on the guitarist's expertise in this style to play what is appropriate and make this "skeleton" chord sketch a viable rhythm guitar part. Being able to have the experience and innate ability to provide the appropriate rhythm (sound and chord voicings) is a skill well worth developing.

II. The second is what an experienced rhythm guitarist would probably play. Remember, there are many different ways these progressions can be executed and the manner in which they are notated is just one option.

III. The third and final example is an advanced method that is becoming a lost art form. The old-school rhythm players like Freddie Green would reharmonize, add chord extensions and do many technical and harmonic variations that could boggle the mind. The amazing aspect is that they did not think of these techniques as reharmonizations or chord substitutions, but played what sounded good to their ears. In many ways, this is the best way to approach any form of music.

**Use only down strokes and try to release pressure (not sound) between each chord.*

LARGE ENSEMBLE SWING

Blues—Basic Rhythm Format (Written)

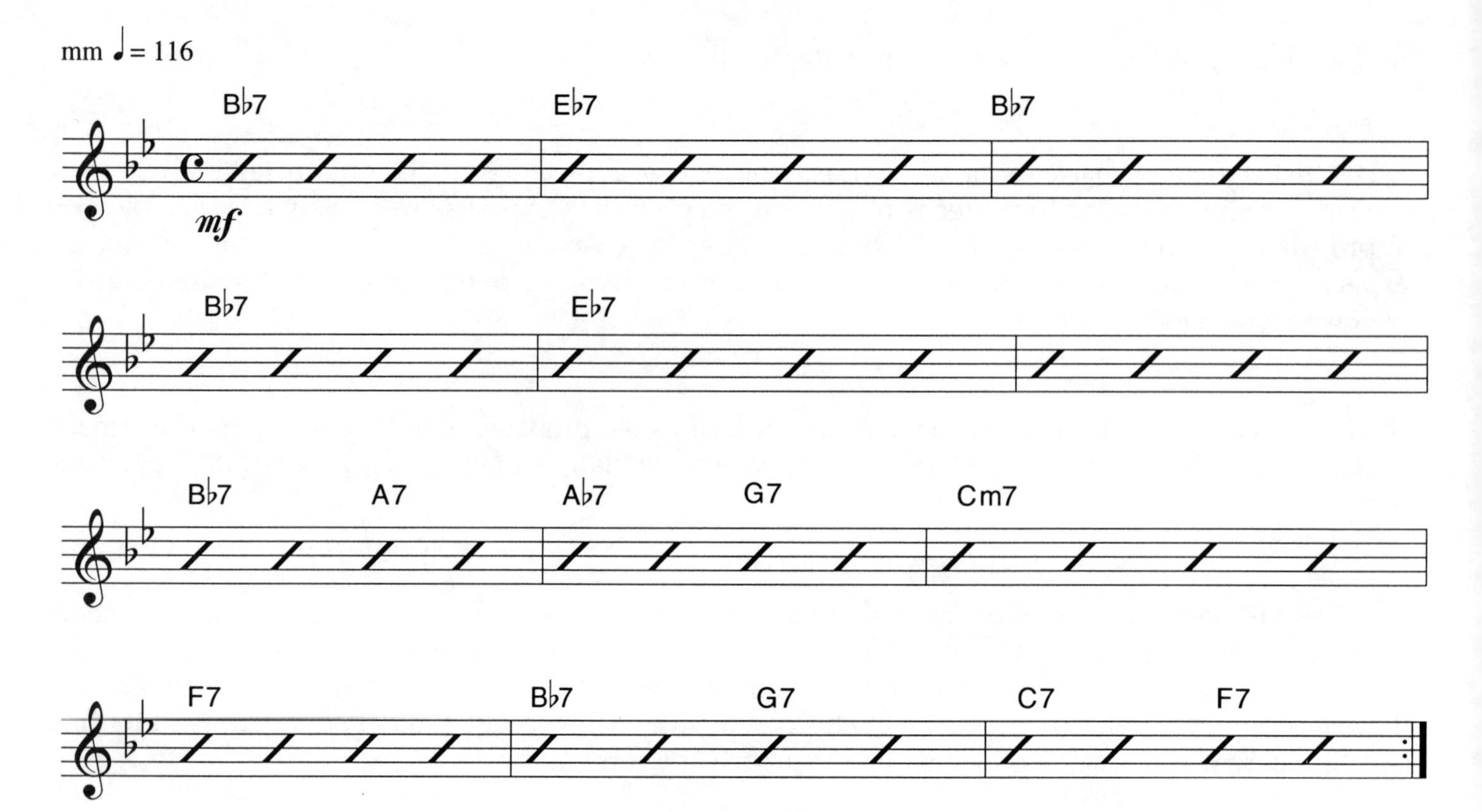

LARGE ENSEMBLE SWING

Blues—Basic Rhythm Format (Played)

LARGE ENSEMBLE SWING

Blues—Rhythm Format (Advanced)

STYLISTIC EXAMPLES

Standard Swing Tune #1—Basic Rhythm Format (As Written)

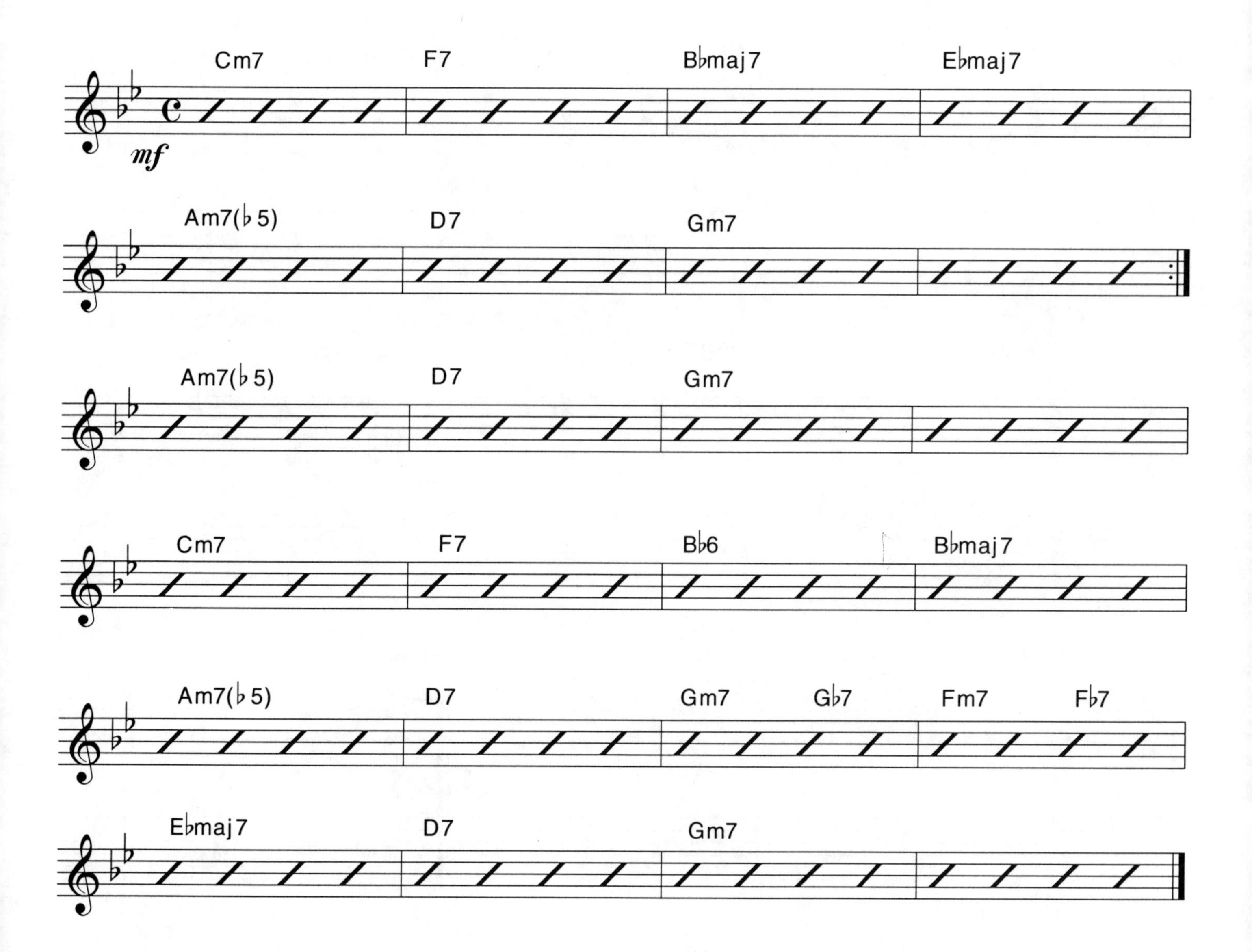

LARGE ENSEMBLE SWING

Standard Swing Tune #1—Basic Rhythm Format (As Played)

LARGE ENSEMBLE SWING

Standard Swing Tune #1—Rhythm Format con't (As Played)

LARGE ENSEMBLE SWING

Standard Swing Tune #1—Rhythm Format (Advanced)

LARGE ENSEMBLE SWING

Standard Swing Tune #1—Rhythm Format con't (Advanced)

LARGE ENSEMBLE SWING

Standard Tune #2 — Basic Rhythm Format (As Written)

Note: When performing in this large ensemble style, the rhythm guitarist will often eliminate chord extensions such as a ♭9 etc. You want to keep the sound uncluttered and just lay down a smooth layer of sound for the rest of the band to play over.

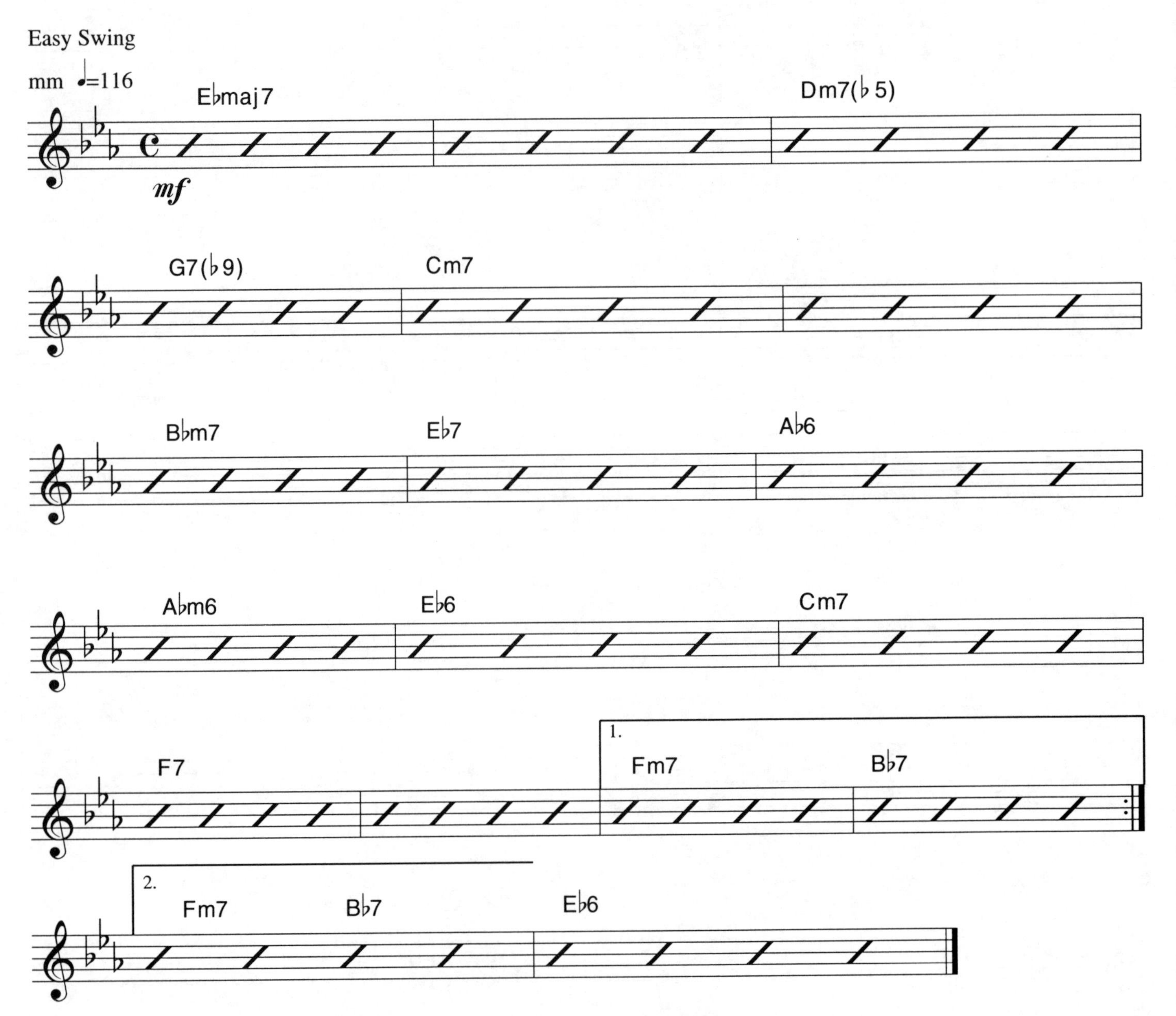

Note this progression in the small band setting (page 36) and how it differs.

LARGE ENSEMBLE SWING

Standard Tune #2 —Rhythm Format (As Played)

LARGE ENSEMBLE SWING

Standard Tune #2 —Rhythm Format (Advanced)

LARGE ENSEMBLE SWING

Standard Tune #3 — Basic Rhythm Format (As Written)

LARGE ENSEMBLE SWING

Standard Tune #3 —Rhythm Format (As Played)

LARGE ENSEMBLE SWING

Standard Tune #3 —Rhythm Format con't (As Played)

LARGE ENSEMBLE SWING

Standard Tune #3 —Rhythm Format (Advanced)

LARGE ENSEMBLE SWING

Standard Tune #3 —Rhythm Format con't (Advanced)

Chapter VI

LARGE ENSEMBLE LATIN

Bossa (As Written)

LARGE ENSEMBLE LATIN

Samba (As Written)

LARGE ENSEMBLE LATIN

Bossa (As Played)

LARGE ENSEMBLE LATIN

Bossa con't—(As Played)

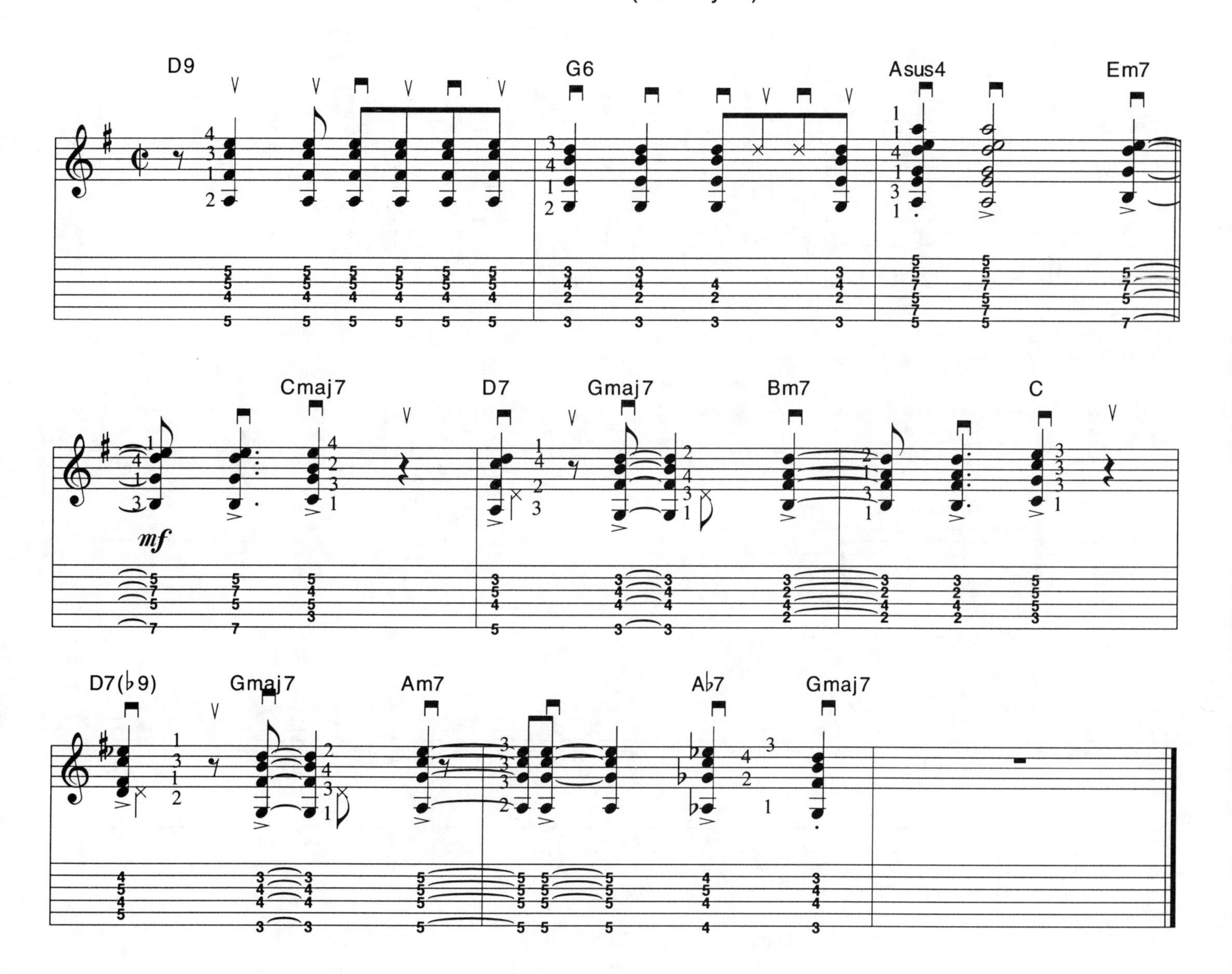

LARGE ENSEMBLE LATIN

Samba (As Played)

LARGE ENSEMBLE LATIN

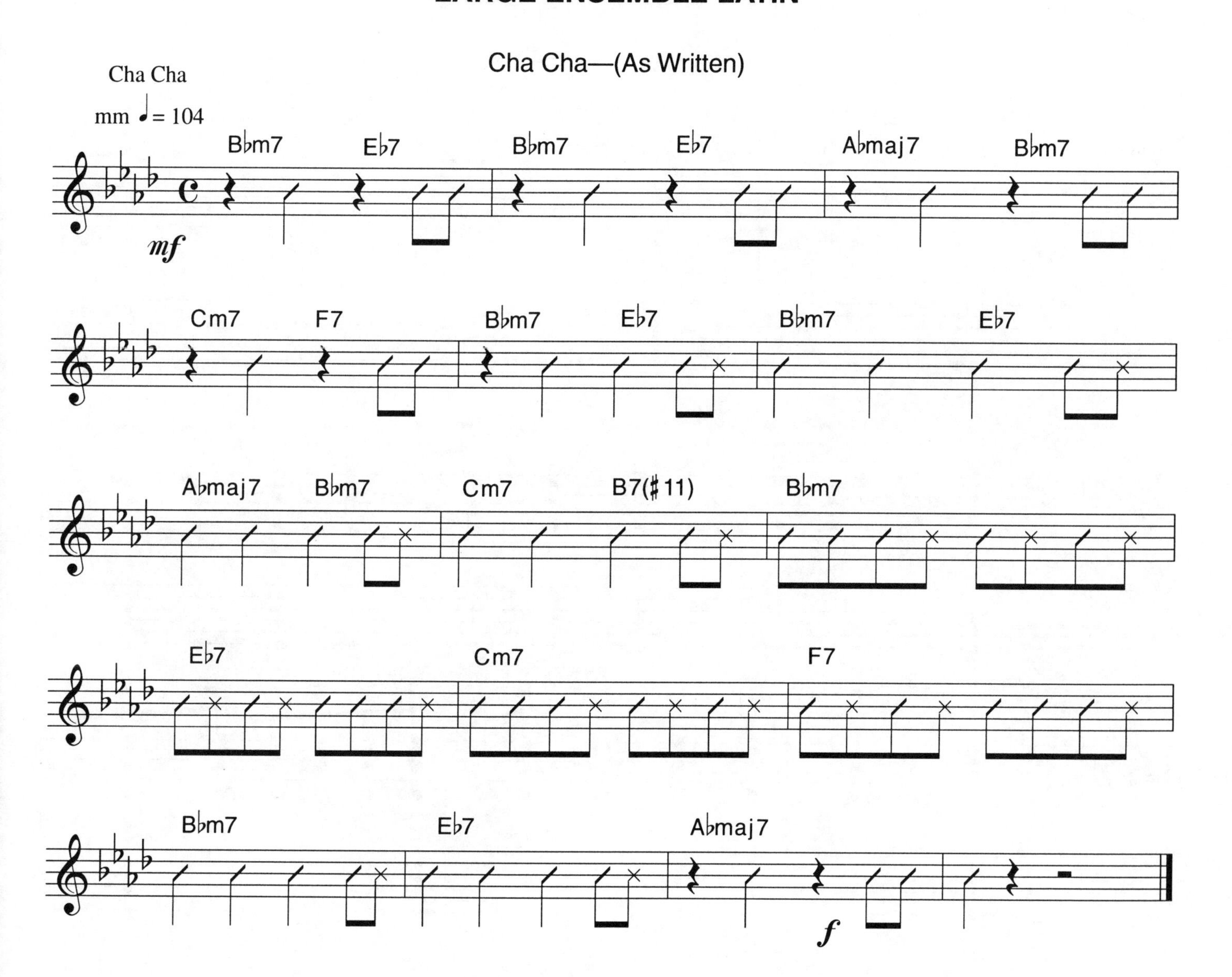

LARGE ENSEMBLE LATIN

Cha Cha—(As Played)

LARGE ENSEMBLE LATIN

Beguine/Rumba Combo—(As Written)

LARGE ENSEMBLE LATIN

Beguine/Rumba Combo—(As Played)

Beguine/Rumba Combo con't—(As Played)

LARGE ENSEMBLE LATIN

Pasa Doble—(As Written)

LARGE ENSEMBLE LATIN

Bolero—(As Written)

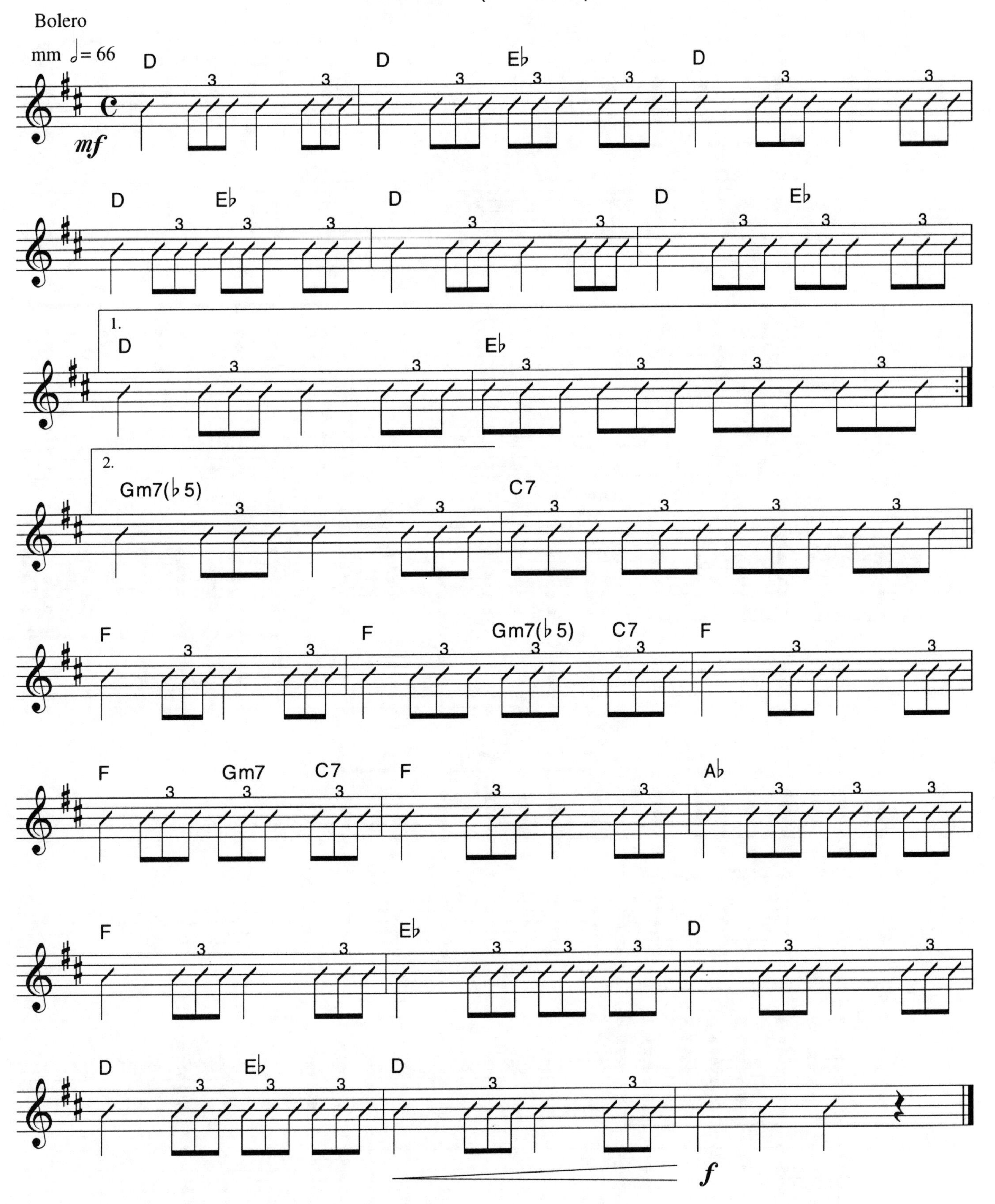

LARGE ENSEMBLE LATIN

Pasa Doble—(As Played)

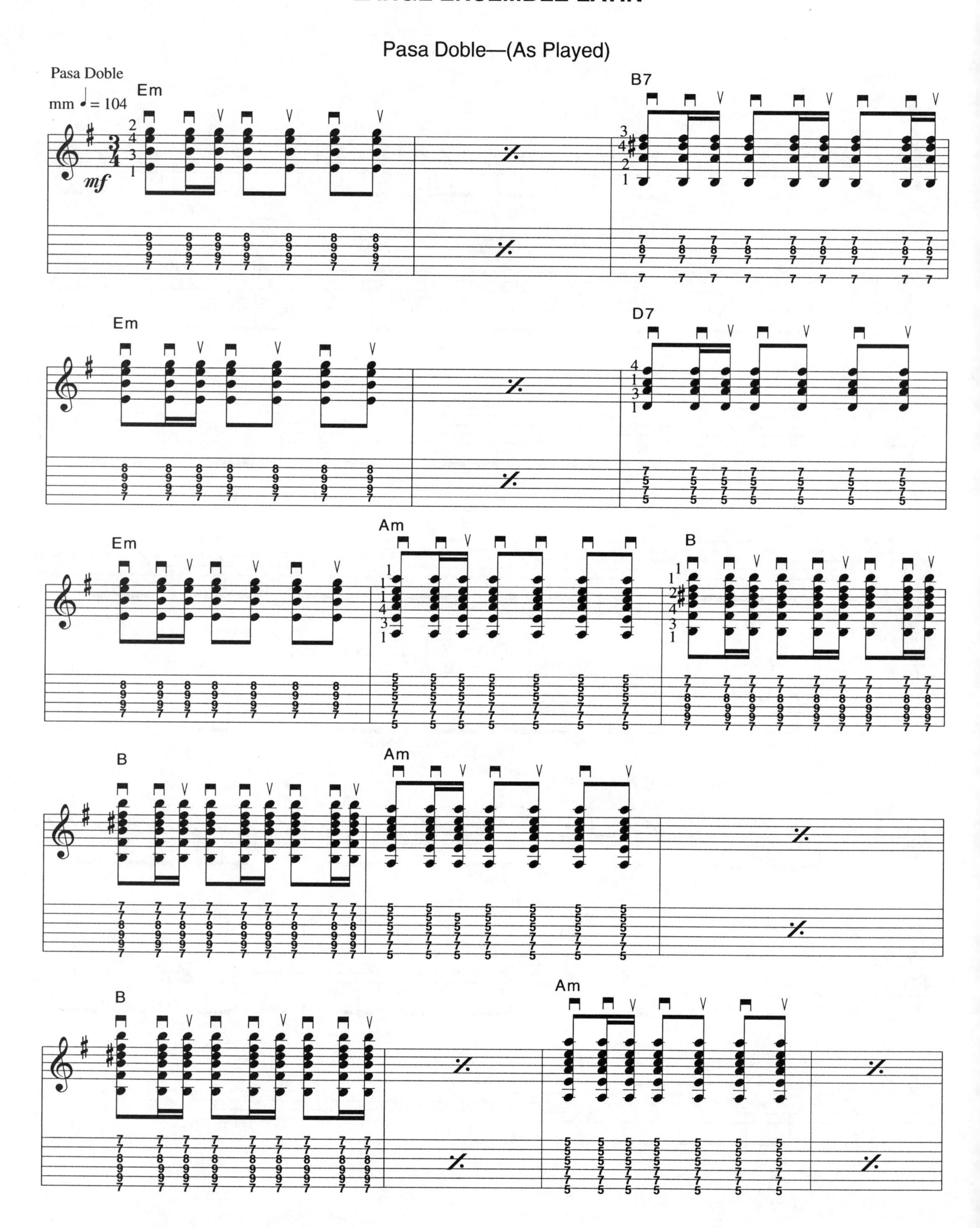

LARGE ENSEMBLE LATIN

Pasa Doble con't—(As Played)

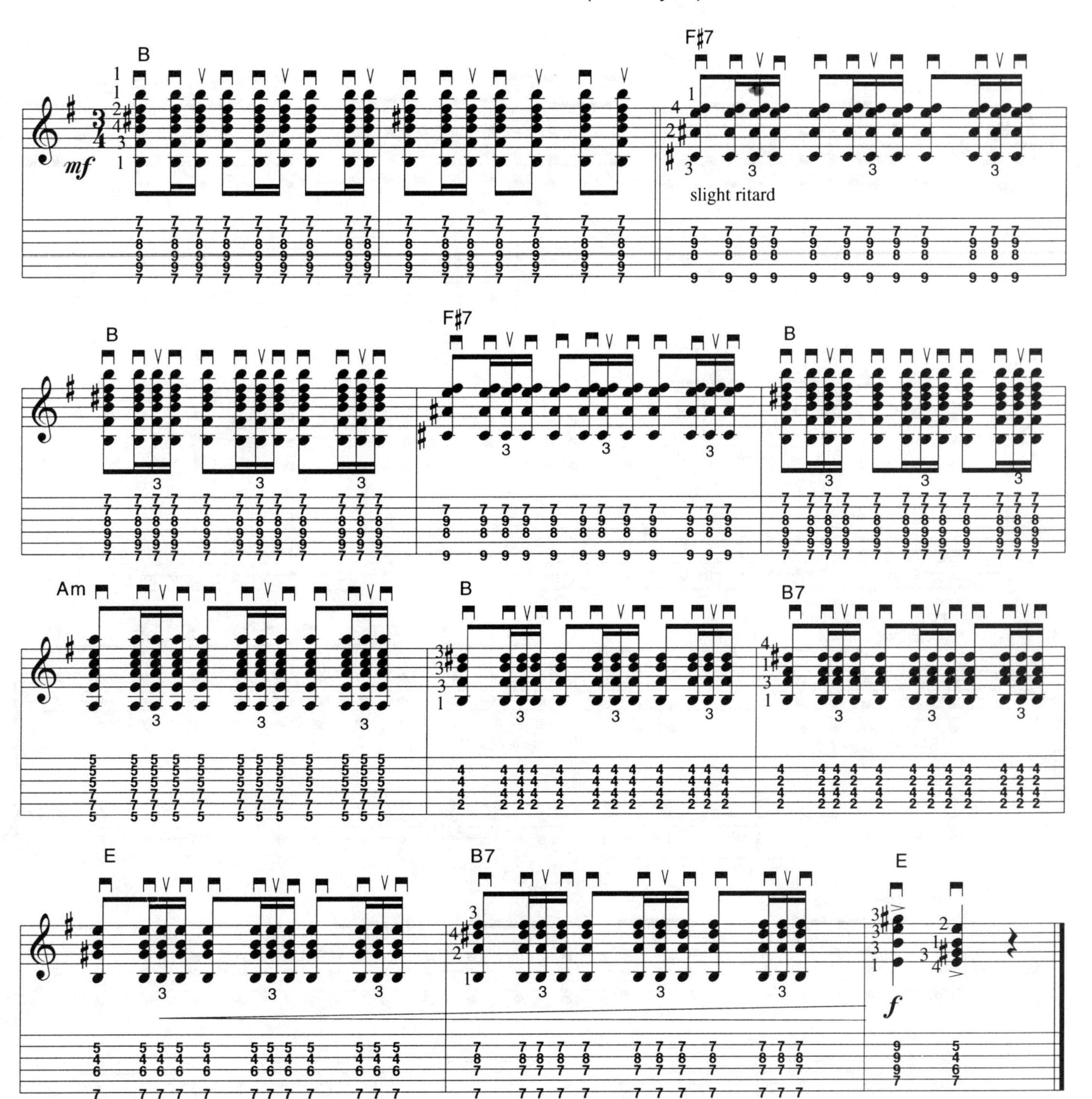

LARGE ENSEMBLE LATIN

Bolero—(As Played)

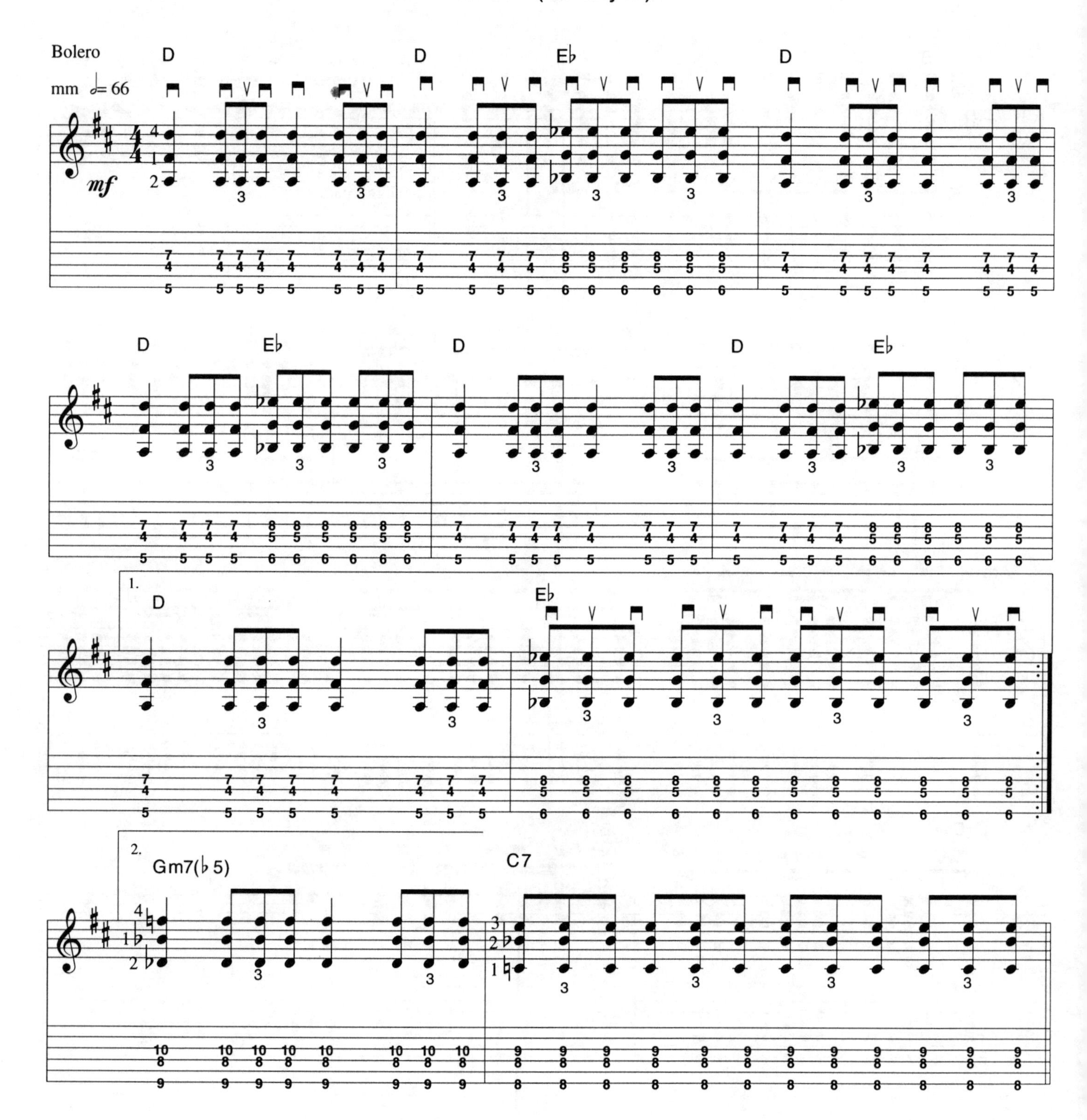

LARGE ENSEMBLE LATIN

Bolero con't—(As Played)

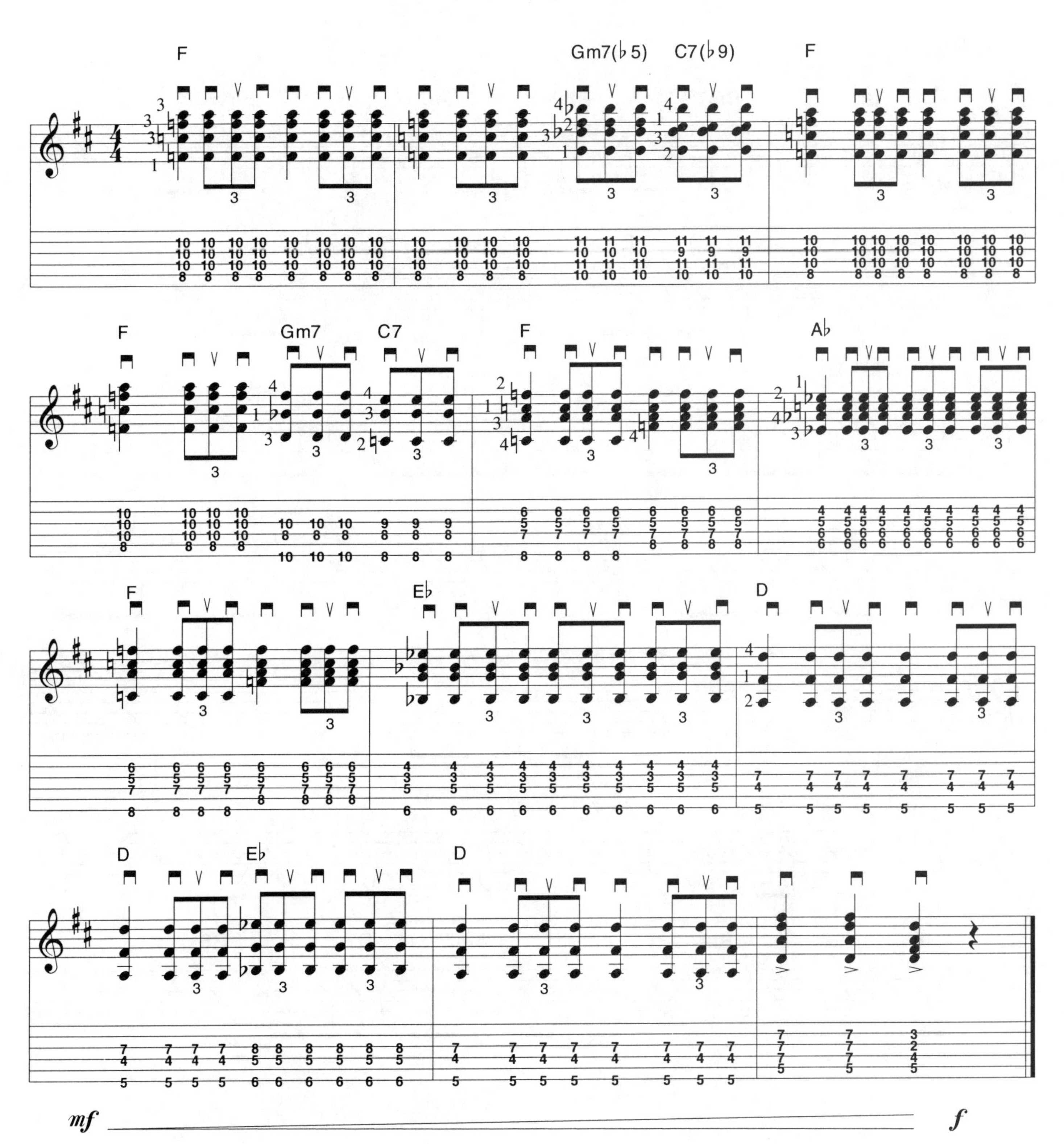

LARGE ENSEMBLE LATIN

Mambo—(As Written)

LARGE ENSEMBLE LATIN

Merenge—(As Written)

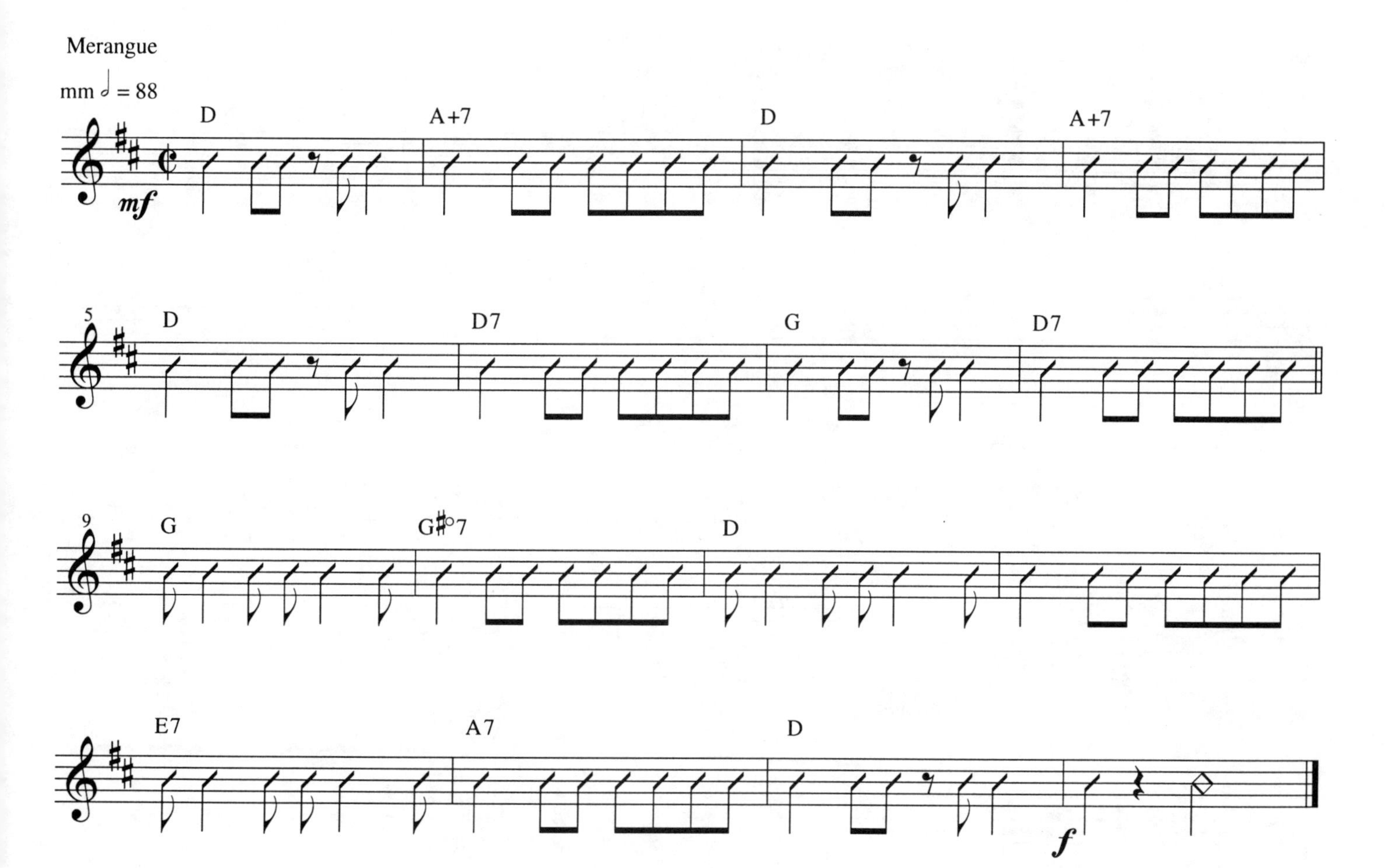

LARGE ENSEMBLE LATIN

Mambo—(As Played)

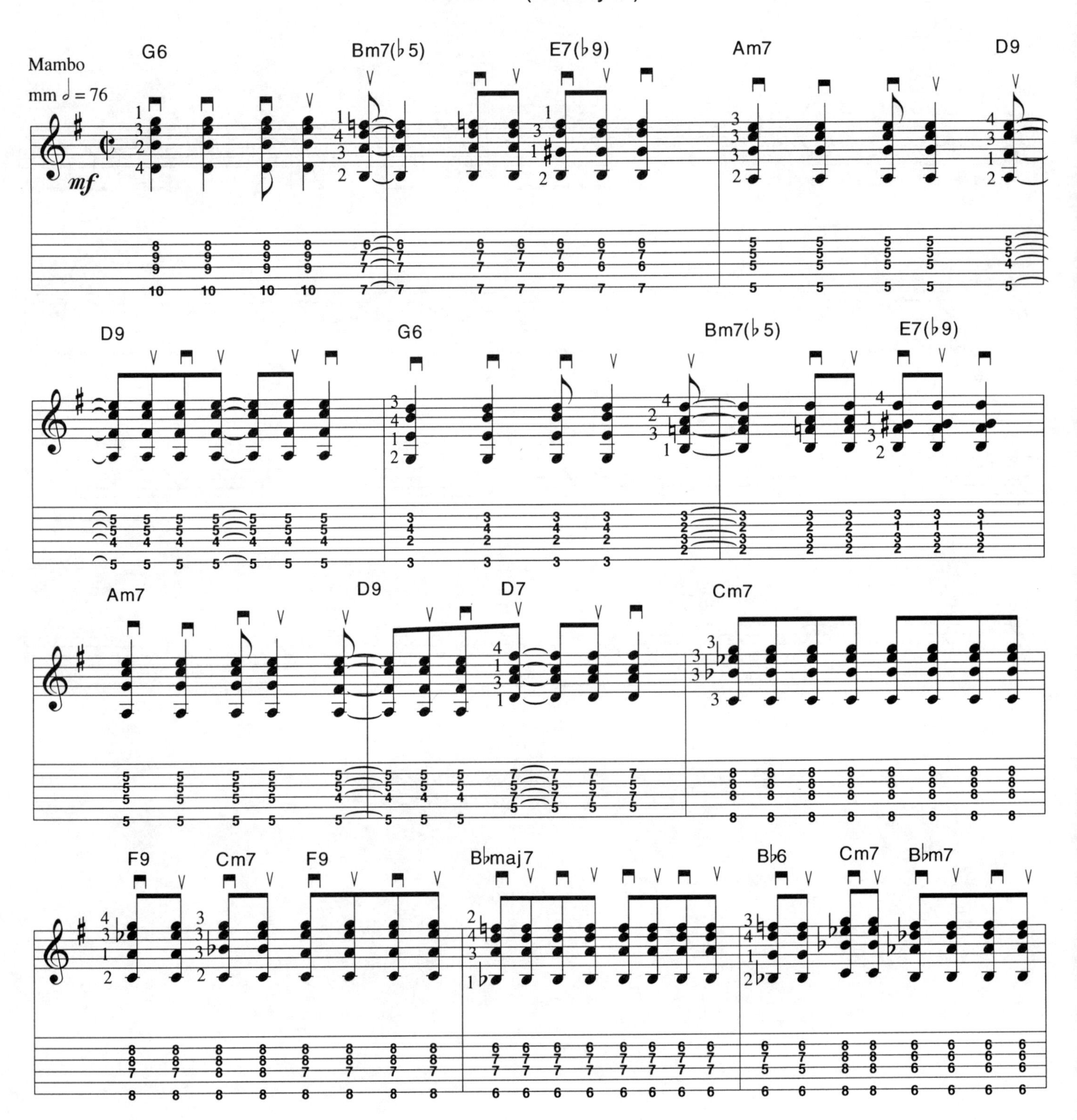

LARGE ENSEMBLE LATIN

Mambo con't—(As Played)

LARGE ENSEMBLE LATIN

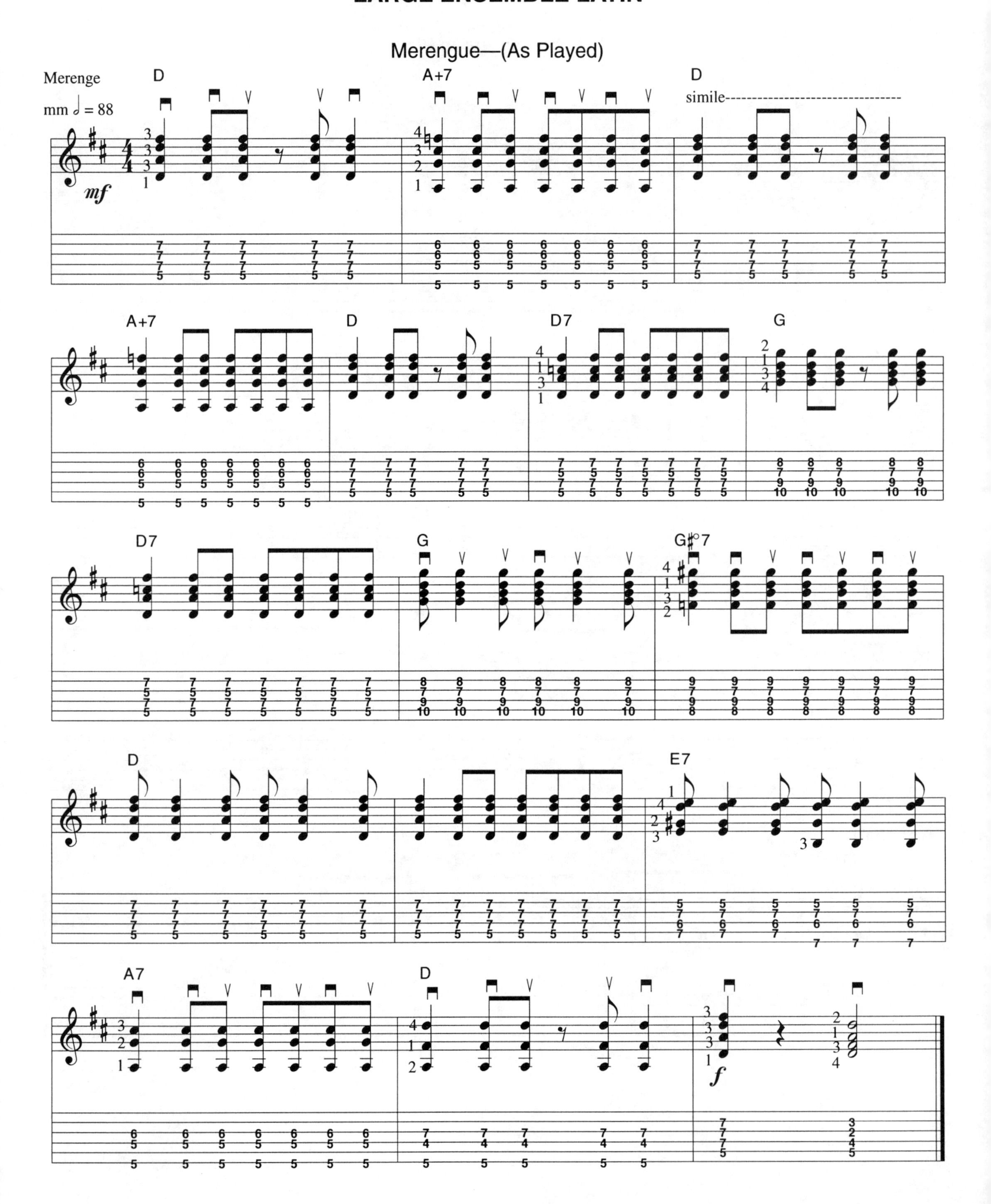

LARGE ENSEMBLE LATIN

Tango—(As Written)

LARGE ENSEMBLE LATIN

Tango—(As Played)

LARGE ENSEMBLE LATIN

Tango con't—(As Played)

Chapter VII

LARGE ENSEMBLE MISCELLANEOUS

Traditional Waltz—(As Written)

**Even though the metronome is slated for quarter notes per minute, the Waltz is generally felt with one pulse per measure.*

LARGE ENSEMBLE MISCELLANEOUS

Traditional Waltz—(As Played)

LARGE ENSEMBLE MISCELLANEOUS

Swing Waltz—(As Written)

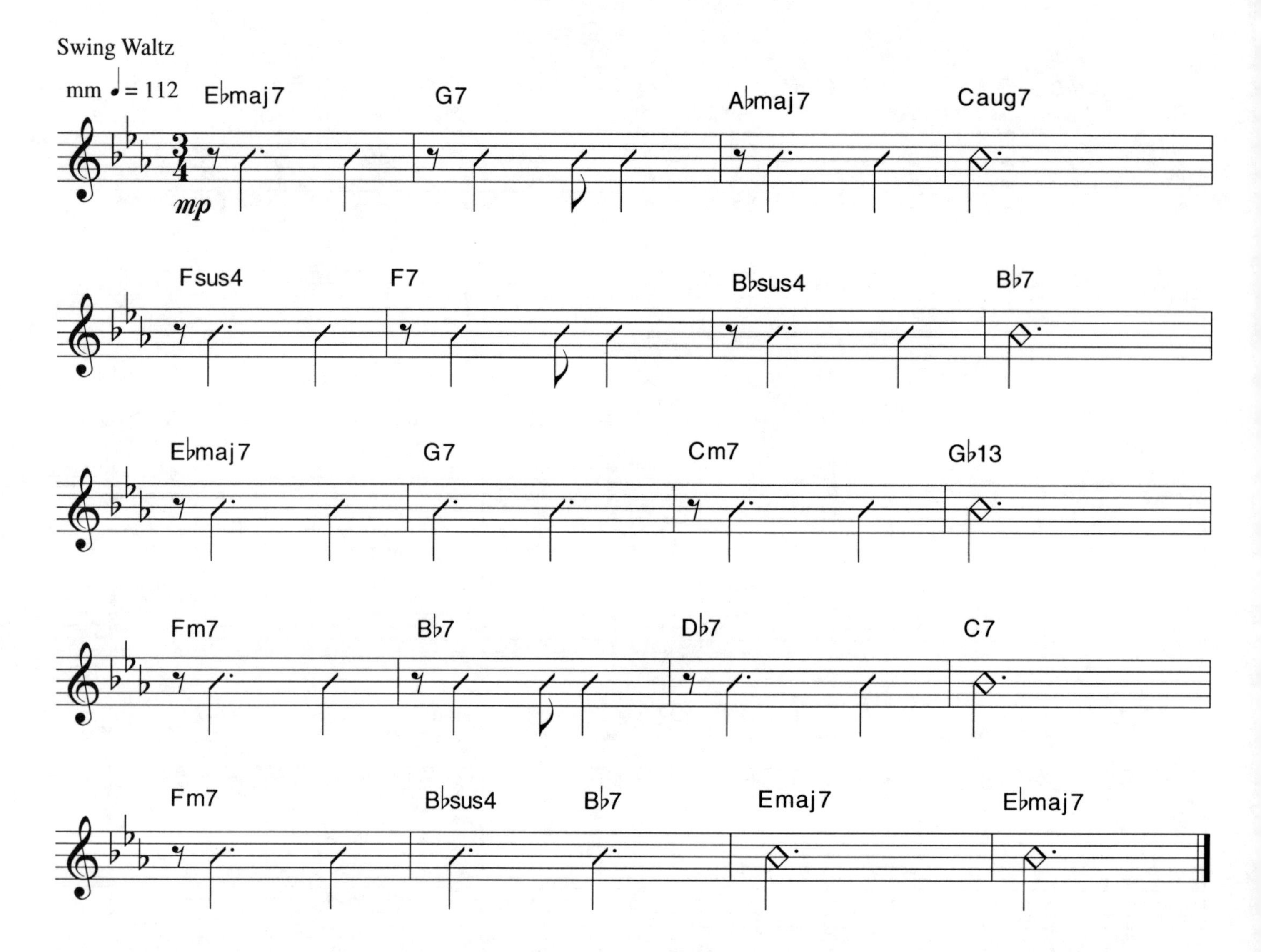

LARGE ENSEMBLE MISCELLANEOUS

Swing Waltz—(As Played)

LARGE ENSEMBLE MISCELLANEOUS

2 to 4—(As Written)

LARGE ENSEMBLE MISCELLANEOUS

2 to 4—(As Played)

V.S. QUICKLY

LARGE ENSEMBLE MISCELLANEOUS

2 to 4 con't—(As Played)

This page has been left blank to avoid awkward page turns.

LARGE ENSEMBLE MISCELLANEOUS

5/4 Swing—(As Written)

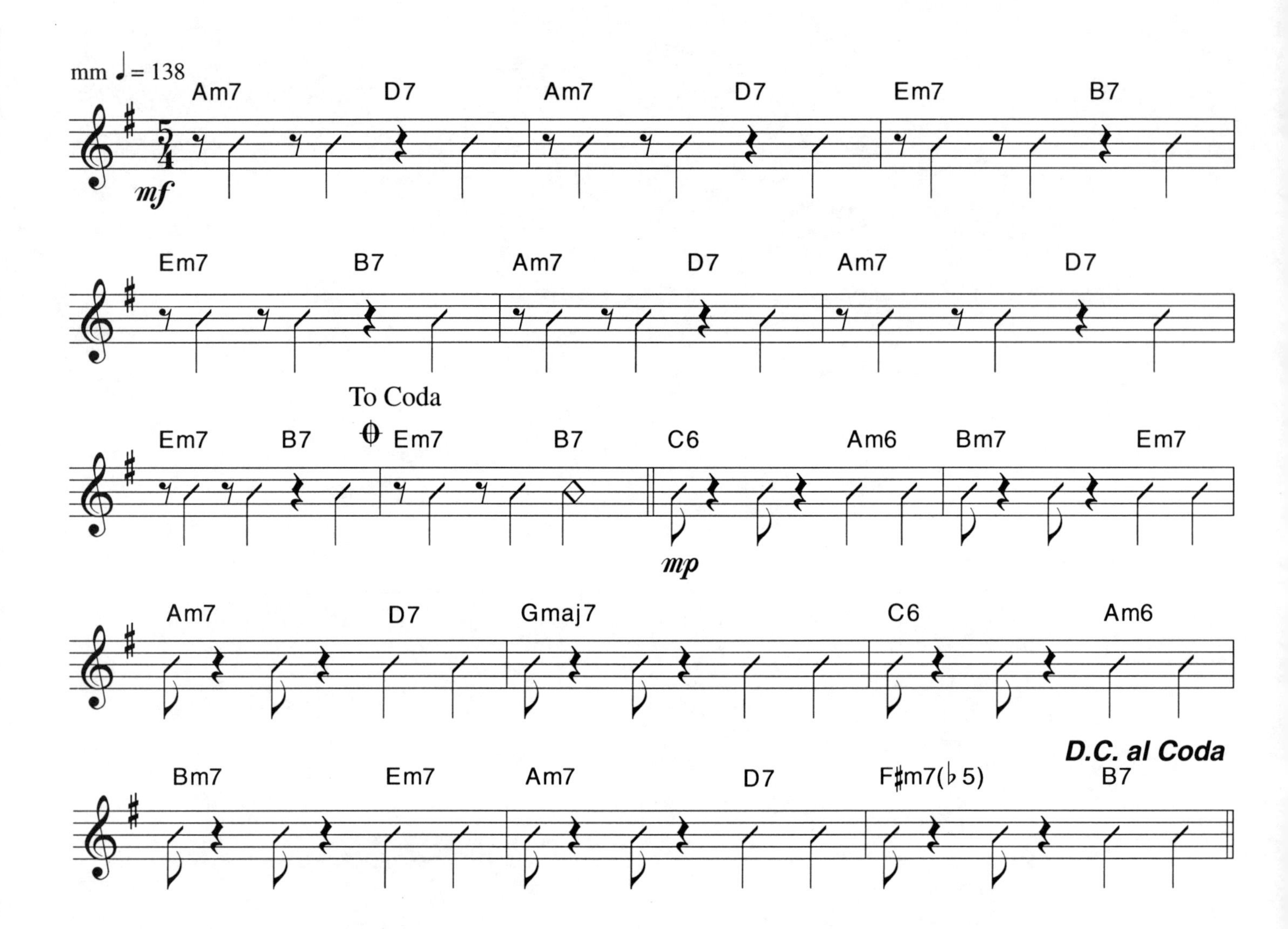

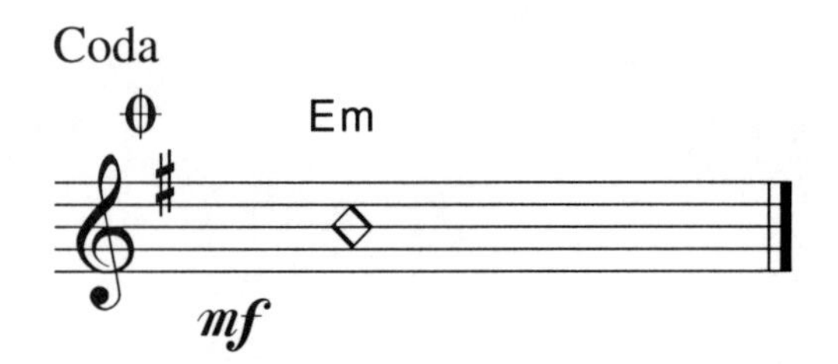

LARGE ENSEMBLE MISCELLANEOUS

5/4 Swing—(As Played)

LARGE ENSEMBLE MISCELLANEOUS

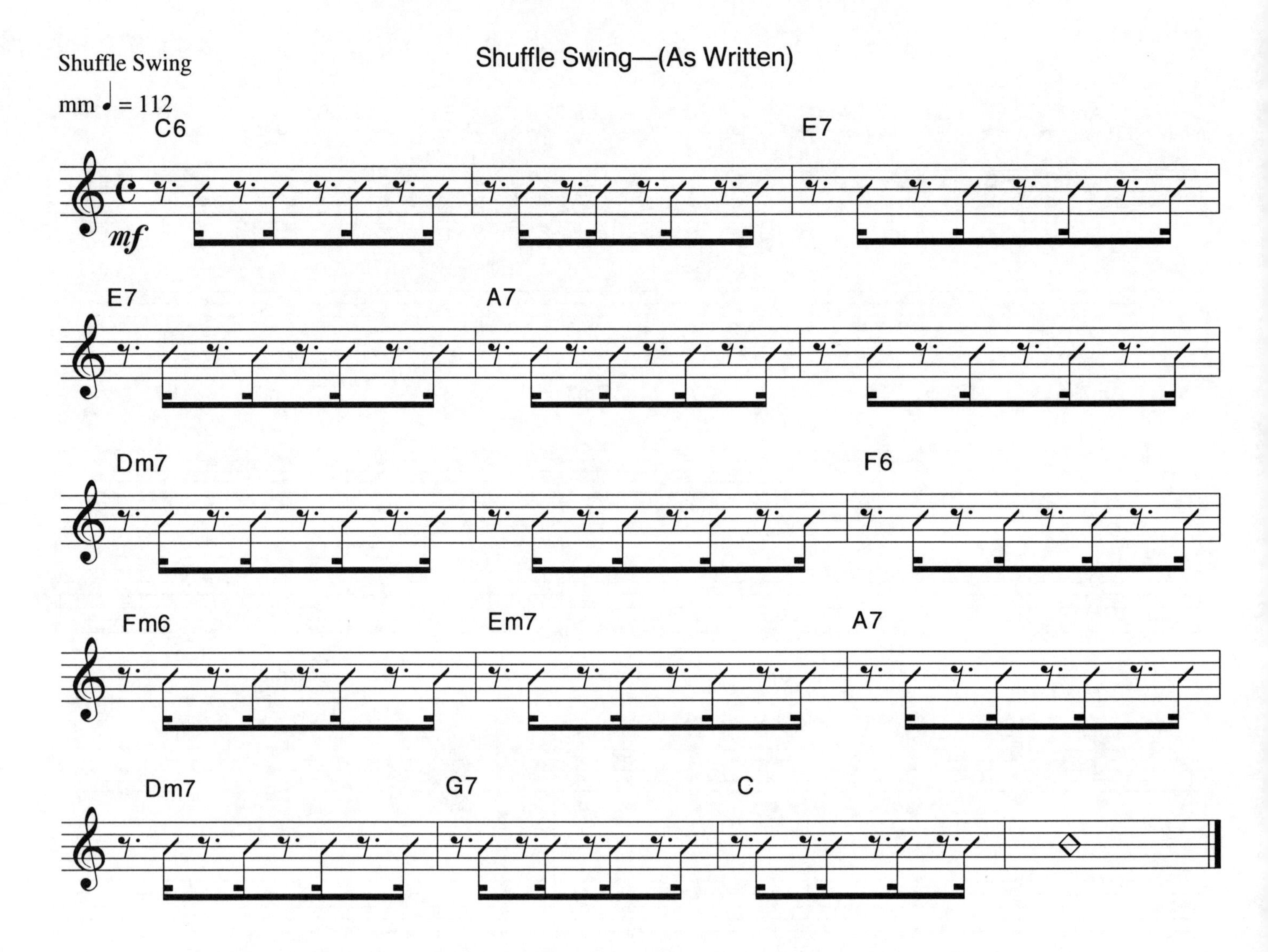

LARGE ENSEMBLE MISCELLANEOUS

Shuffle Swing—(As Played)

In this idiom, this is how the shuffle is usually indicated, although a triplet (swing) feel is usually what is desired.

LARGE ENSEMBLE MISCELLANEOUS

Rhythm Potpourri—(As Written)

V.S. QUICKLY

LARGE ENSEMBLE MISCELLANEOUS

Rhythm Potpourri cont'—(As Written)

LARGE ENSEMBLE MISCELLANEOUS

Rhythm Potpourri cont'—(As Written)

V.S. QUICKLY

LARGE ENSEMBLE MISCELLANEOUS

Rhythm Potpourri cont'—(As Played)

LARGE ENSEMBLE MISCELLANEOUS

Rhythm Potpourri cont'—(As Played)

V.S. QUICKLY

LARGE ENSEMBLE MISCELLANEOUS

Rhythm Potpourri cont'—(As Played)

Chapter VIII

RHYTHM GUITAR—by the numbers

Basic Principal

To be able to play any chord progression in any key is paramount to being a good rhythm guitarist. This was a very difficult technique for me to learn until a seasoned guitarist took me aside and told me the secret of the pros. It's all by the numbers!

The basic premise is to use the numeric function instead of the letter name to identify a chord. For example, in the key of C:

C =1
D = 2
E = 3
etc.

The next step is to train your hands and mind to think this way. It takes a little while to get your reaction time together, but once you get it going, it is a very easy task to play any common chord progression, in any key, without a second thought.

Example:

Example above translated to the number system:

* *Roman numerals are commonly used to denote the number (function) of the chord structure.*

RHYTHM GUITAR—by the numbers

Basic Principal—con't

When chords are altered from the basic structure, simply add the extension:

RHYTHM GUITAR—by the numbers

Nashville Number System

Rhythm guitarists in all genres have used this method for years, but many consider it a Nashville invention. In fact, many refer to this as the "Nashville Number System".

The chord charts can go from the very simplistic to the extremely complicated with it's downfall being that it is not standardized.

When this numeric arrangement is referred to as the "Nashville System" only arabic numbers are used. Often, in the Nashville studios, number charts (like below) are often handed out in place of a chord chart.

Example #1—Basic Number System Chart

1 6m 4 5^7 4 4m 5 5^7

4 6m 2m 5^7 1 6m 4 5 1

Example #2—Basic Number System Chart

|| 1 | 6m | 4 | 5^7 || 4 | 4m | 5 | | ||

|| 4 | 6m | 2m7 | 5^7 || 1 | 6m | 4 5 | 1 ||

Example #1 is a little too simplistic for my sensibilities. It relies on the fact that the rhythm guitarist either has heard the tune and is aware of the harmony or must listen closely to the other musicians (especially the bass) to hear when each chord comes in. Example #2 is what I prefer. It instructs the guitarist when the chords change and just makes sense. In many cases, consider yourself lucky to even get as much as example #1.

Tablature, chord diagrams and the number system are all great tools to be used along with traditional notation. All guitarists, in any genre, should be able to understand the traditional music system that all instruments, in all parts of the world, have used for centuries.

RHYTHM GUITAR—by the numbers

Jazz Numerology

Transposition by the numbers has always been a mainstay among Jazz musicians, but often can get overexuberant and produce complicated monstrosities that are very difficult to understand. When it becomes more of a hindrance than a help, it is time to rethink why you are even using this system. The idea is to come up with a method that makes it easy for you to hear and remember the harmony and be able to play it on your instrument.

Except for Nashville, Roman numerals are always used and rarely is a performer given the numerals to read as a chart. Jazz numerology is generally just a transposition tool and is not something used as a written piece of music.

In the following pages, I am going to provide examples of common progressions and my own personal thought process of how I would remember them. The idea is to look at the number chart and use it as a transposition tool. After a while, when you read a piece of music, you will recognize the numbers without writing it down and be able transpose it in your head. Do not rush this process and use the number chart for as long as necessary.

The most important aspect of playing chords and transposing is being able to hear the progression. If you can't do that, everything else is just a waste of time. A former instructor once told me that before you ever play a melody or try to improvise over a tune you should play the chord progression 50 times. I think this might be a little overkill, but the premise is correct.

Be aware that this method will work for most chord progressions, but you may occasionally come across a tune that changes key many times and uses very complicated harmonic structures that will make this method not only difficult, but impossible. When this happens, all you can do is try to hear the chords and find them on your instruments in anyway possible. There is really no right or wrong way with this method. All that counts is that you can get your hands and ears on the chords that sound good. When you think about it, that's pretty much our goal with everything we do in music.

The golden rule in music is do not let it cease to be fun. Learning to play an instrument is hard work and there is no way around it, but it is also a wonderful outlet for creativity and a sense of self-worth throughout your entire life—so don't let the mechanical frustrations get you down.

Take the technical side of this art form in small doses and always make sure that your music stays fun!

RHYTHM GUITAR—by the numbers

Blues #1

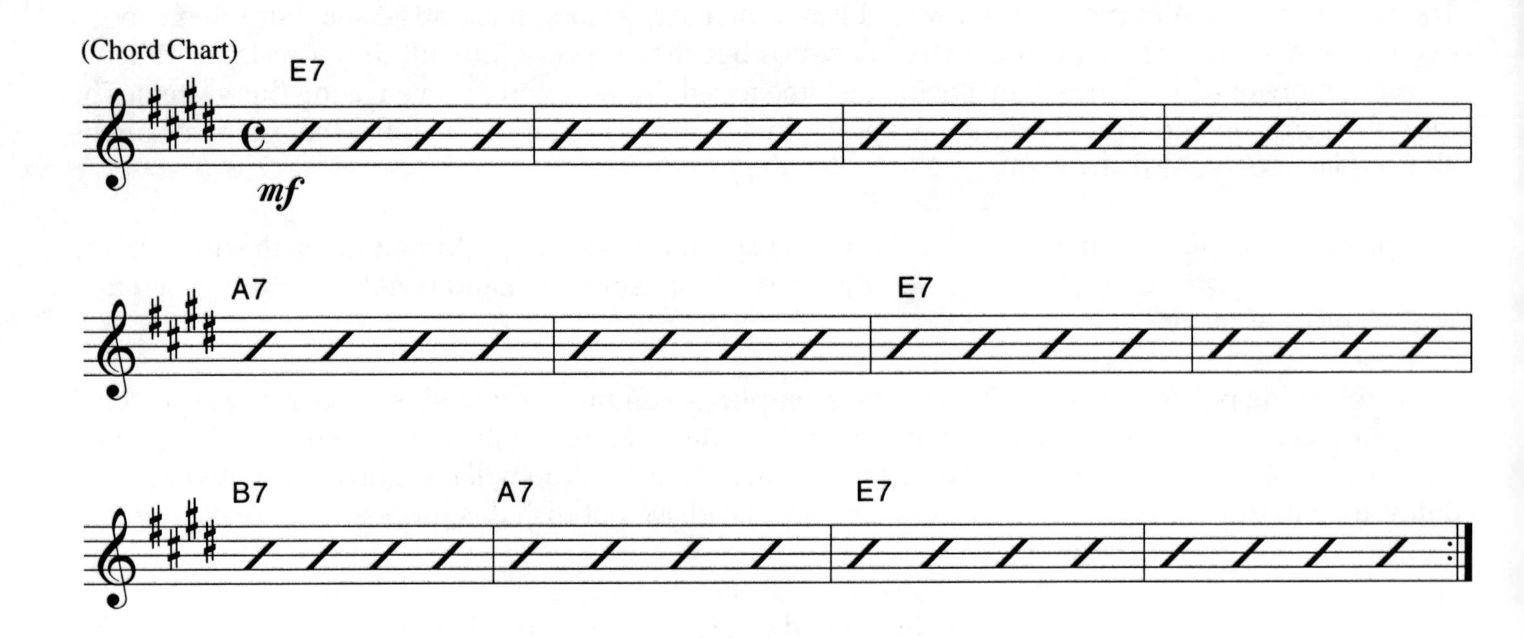

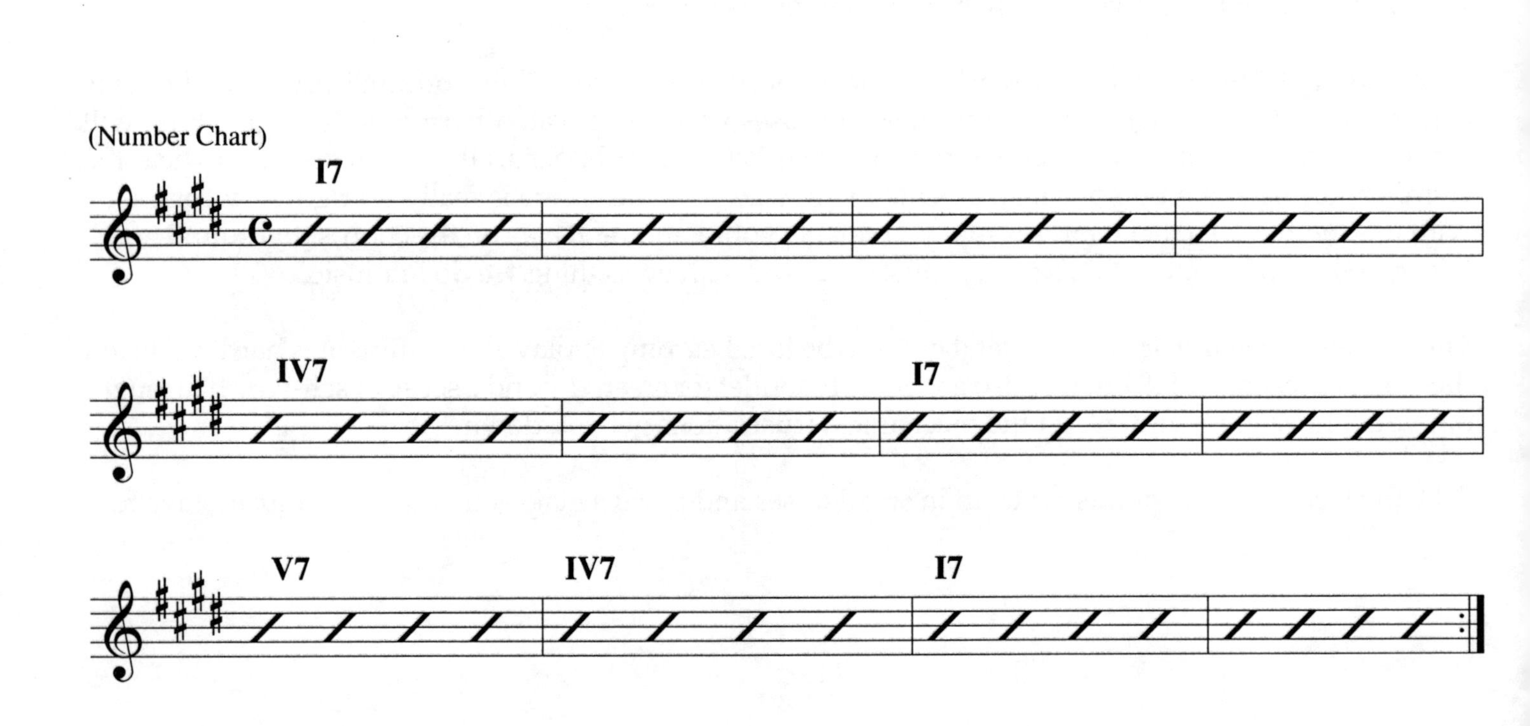

RHYTHM GUITAR—by the numbers

Blues #2

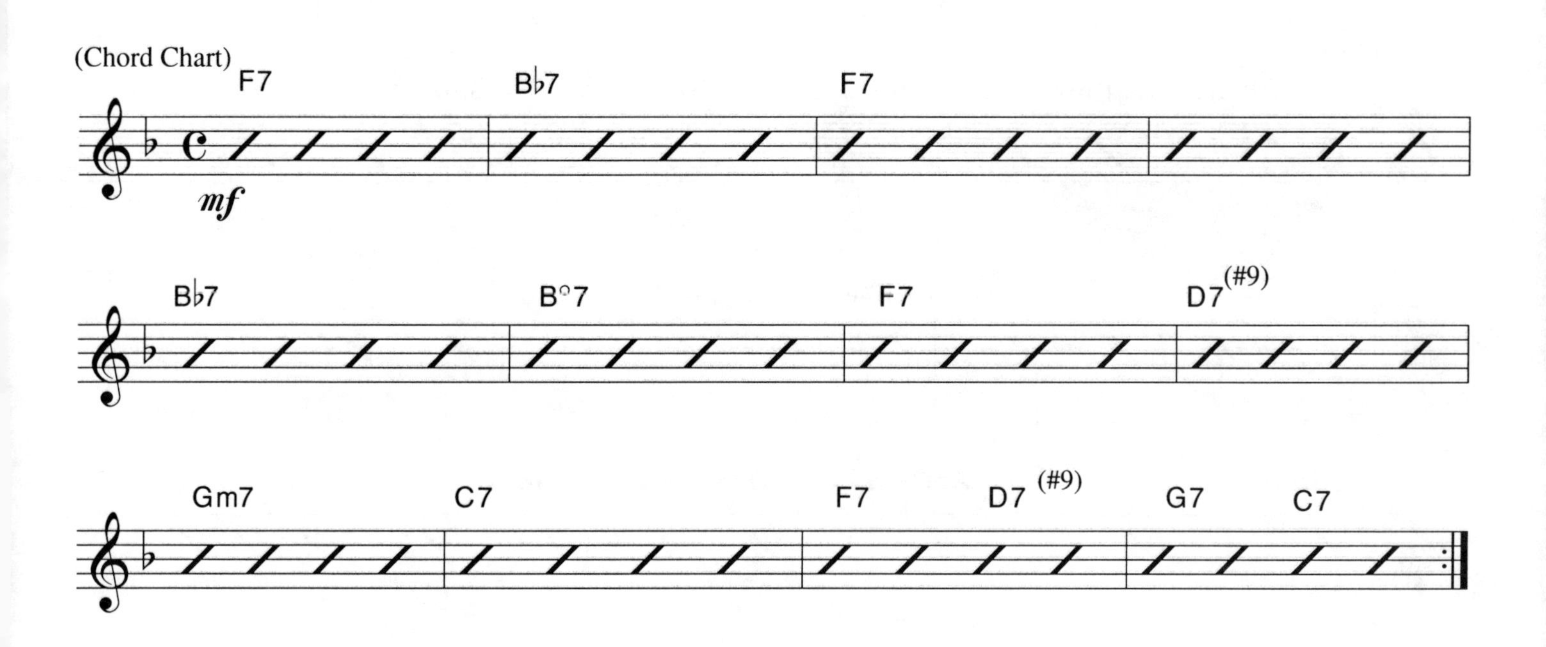

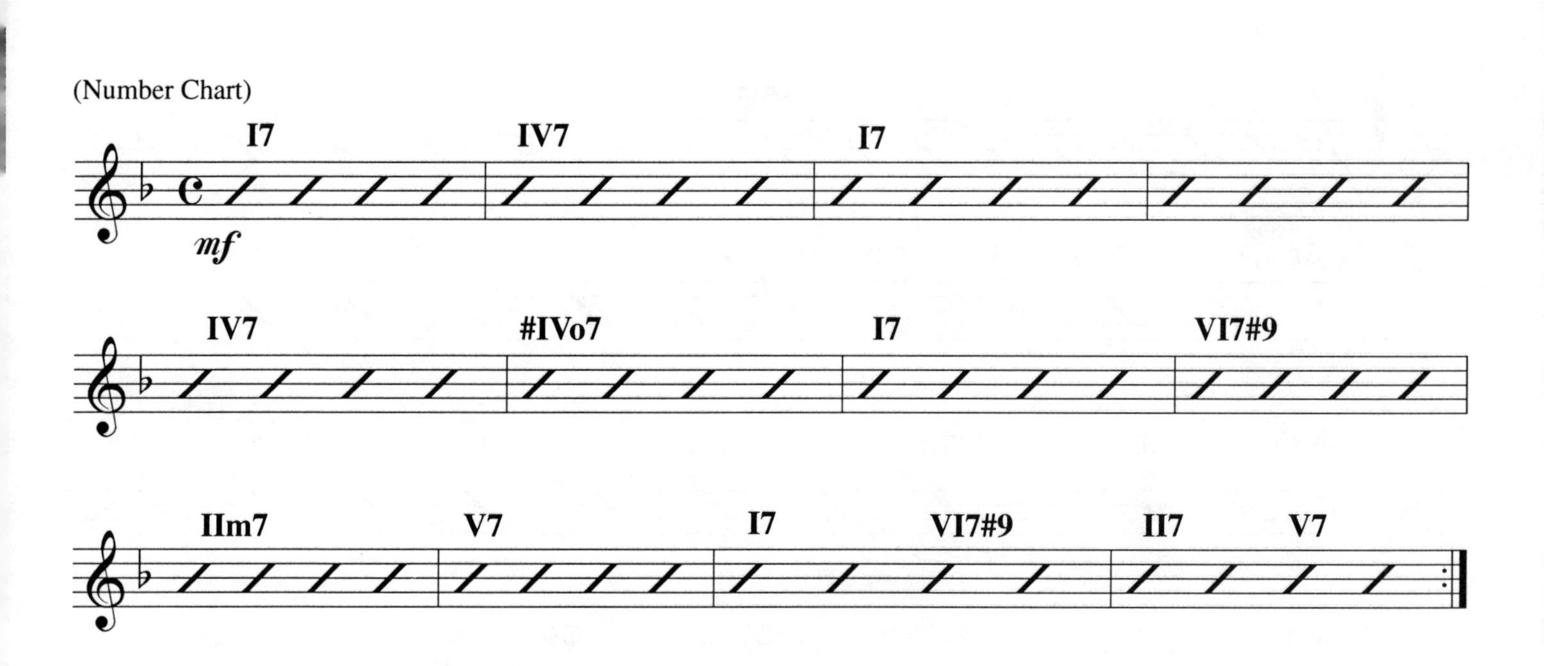

RHYTHM GUITAR—by the numbers

You Got Rhythm

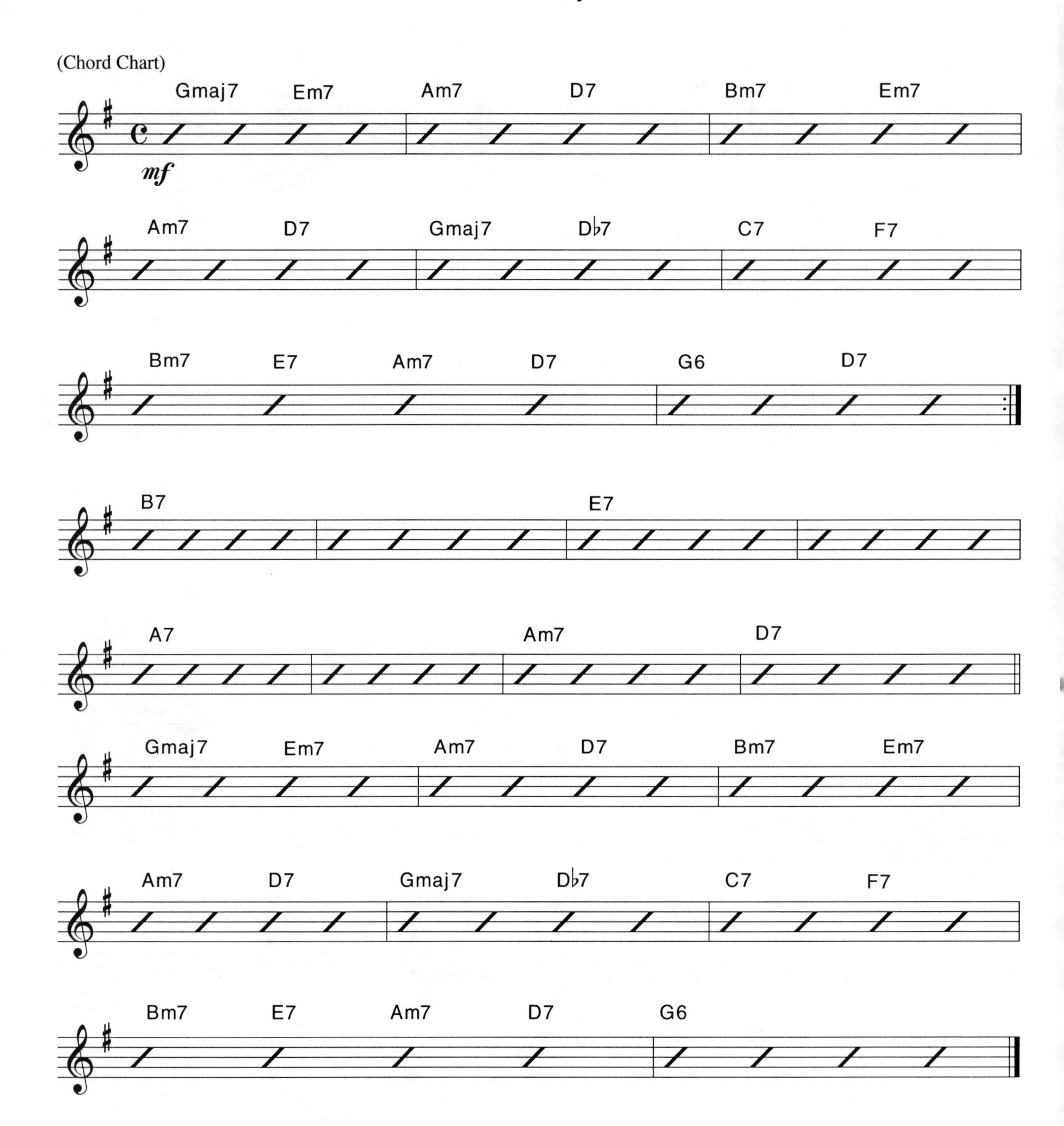

RHYTHM GUITAR—by the numbers

You Got Rhythm

(Number Chart)

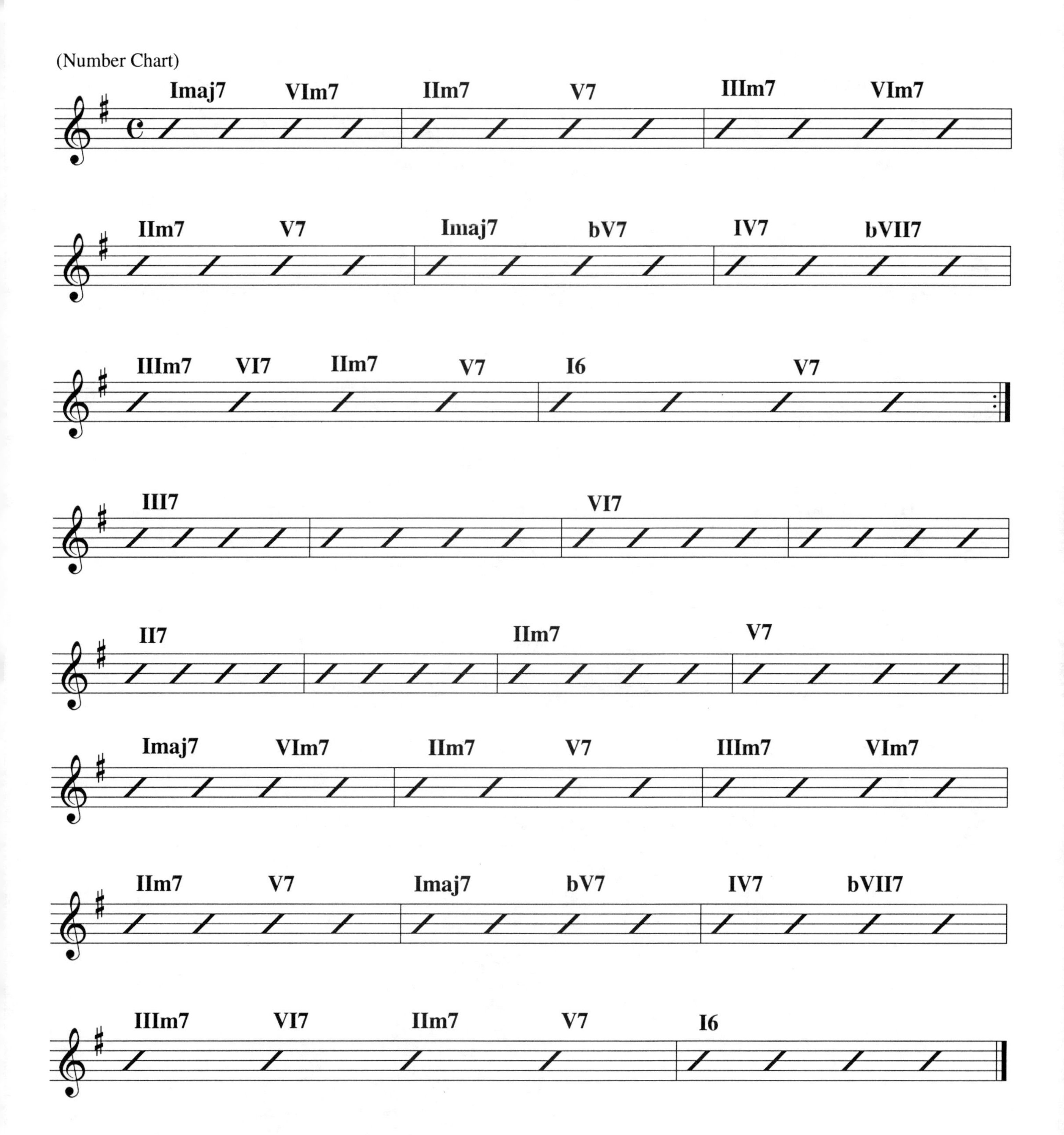

RHYTHM GUITAR—by the numbers

Groovebird

(Chord Chart)

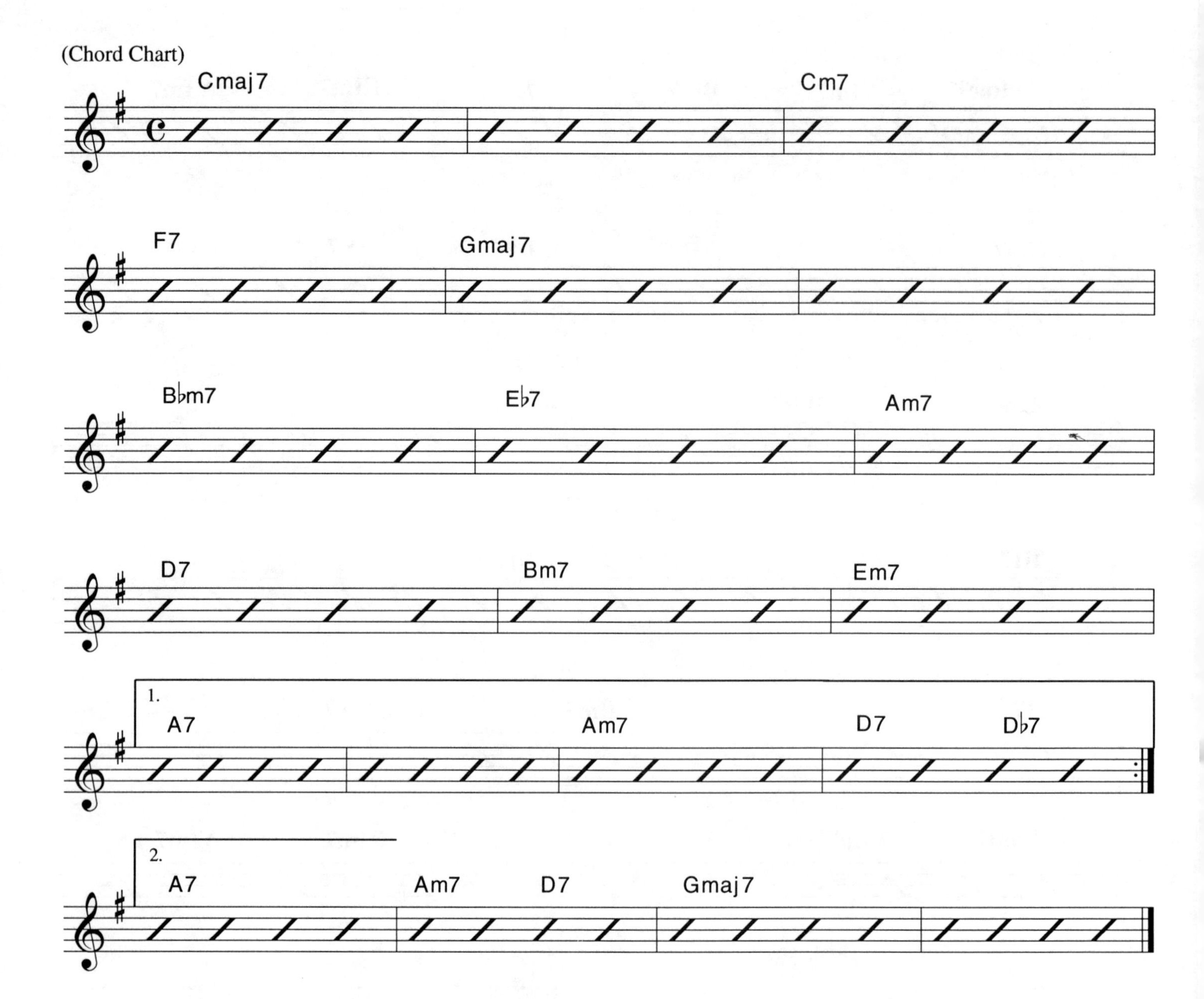

RHYTHM GUITAR—by the numbers

Groovebird

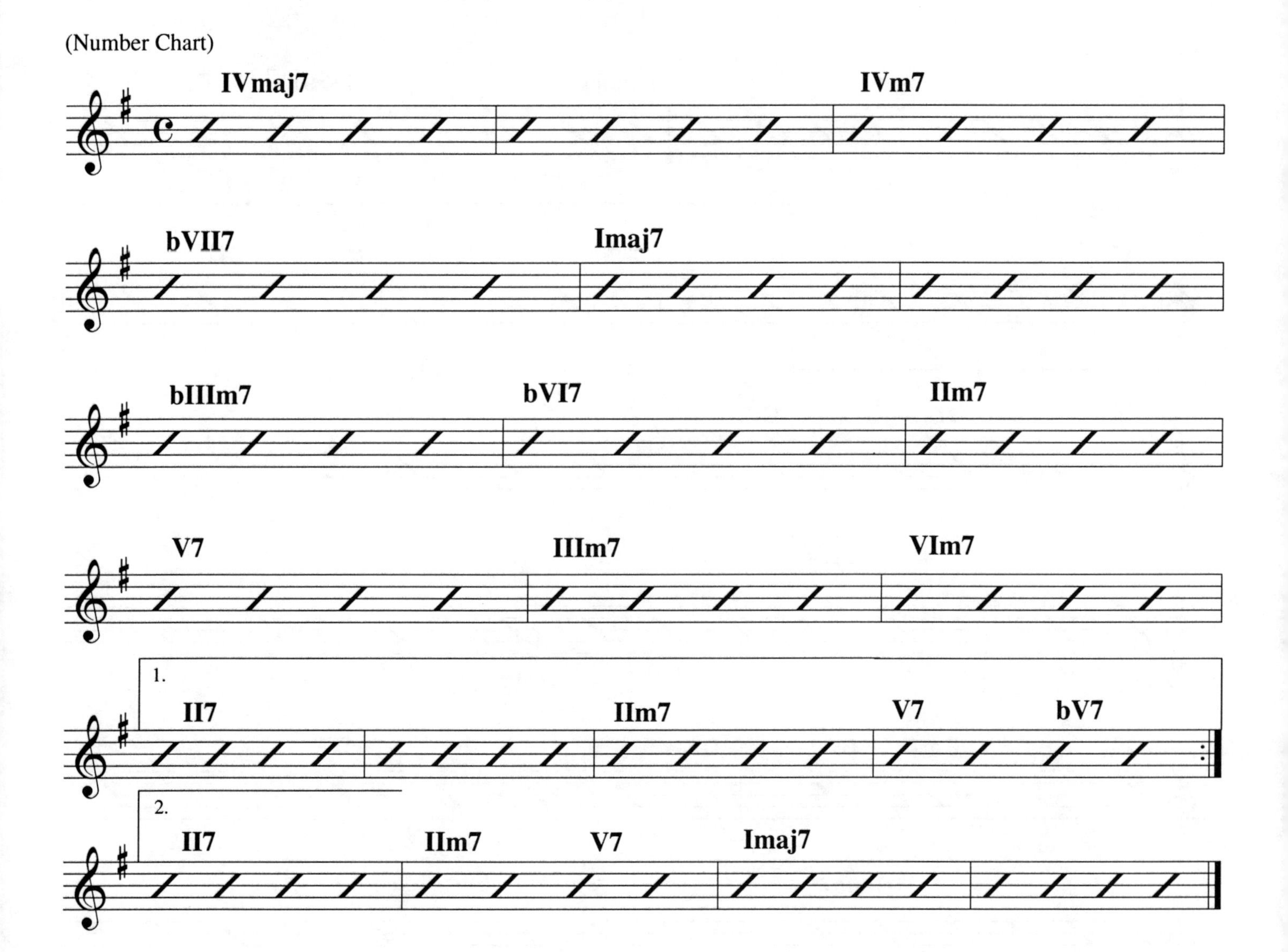

RHYTHM GUITAR—by the numbers

Latin Horizon

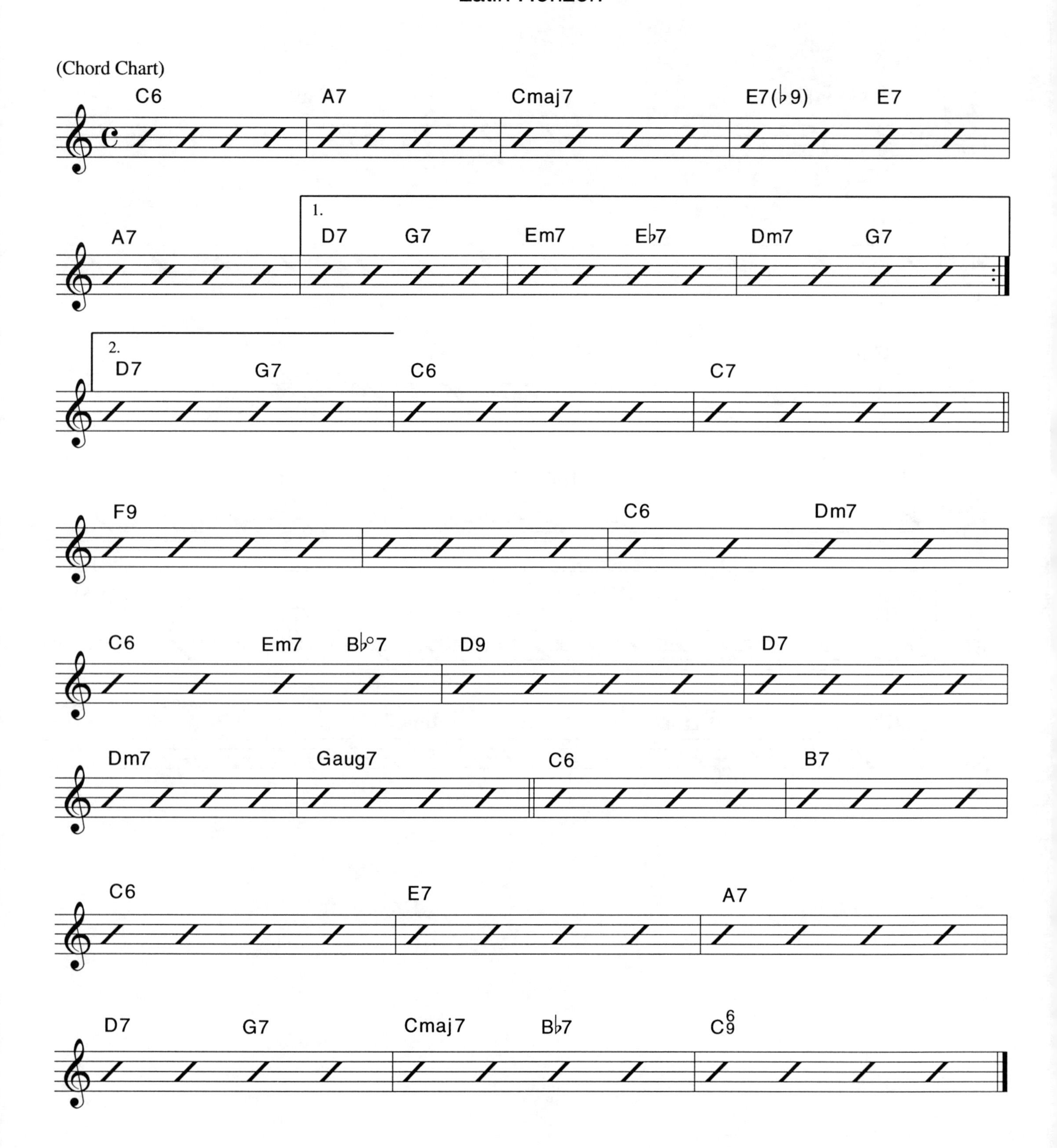

RHYTHM GUITAR—by the numbers

Latin Horizon

(Number Chart)

SUMMARY

I hope you have enjoyed the many varied rhythm guitar styles that are encompassed in this text. Most rhythms in this book have come from actual gig, theater, "dance band" or studio situations I have encountered during my thirty year plus career. I have found that the way you approach the right hand picking technique is paramount to getting the appropriate sound for the situation. A good deal of time and thought has been given to the fingering and picking to provide the appropriate sound and groove. Even though it may seem awkward, there are distinct reasons for it to be executed in the prescribed manner. Please give it a chance before altering the fingering, chord voicing or notated picking.

1971 the famed composer/arranger Burt Bachrach stated to my former teacher and friend, Bill Leavitt, "I always keep a rhythm guitarist on salary because I can find a good lead player (one who reads single notes and improvises) in any major city in the world, but good rhythm guitarists are hard to find." Recently I interviewed the great jazz guitarist Bucky Pizzarelli and his parting words to me were, "I always tell anyone who wants to play guitar to listen to the chords. Before you ever try to play a solo understand and get a "feel" for the harmony. I have made my living backing up people and continue to work because of this facet of guitar playing. My best advice to any guitar player, in any style, is to learn how to play rhythm guitar and learn how the chords work, and everything else will fall in place."

I have thoroughly enjoyed putting this text together and hopefully, you have found it mentally and physically challenging. No matter how the industry, music or technology changes, a good rhythm guitarist cannot be replaced—so have fun and always keep the music in you life.